Oldham Athletic, An A–Z

by Dean Hayes

Palatine Books, 1994

Oldham Athletic, An A–Z

by Dean Hayes

Palatine Books, 1994

Oldham Athletic, An A–Z
by Dean Hayes

Published by Palatine Books,
an imprint of Carnegie Publishing Ltd, 18 Maynard Street, Preston

Typeset in Monotype Ehrhardt by Carnegie Publishing, Preston
Printed in the UK by T. Snape & Co., Preston

British Library Cataloguing-in-Publication Data
A catalogue record for this book is available from the British Library
ISBN 1–874181–12–8

Contents

Abandoned Matches

An abandoned match may be defined as one that is called off by the referee, *whilst it is in progress*, because conditions do not permit it to be completed.

Generally speaking, far fewer matches are abandoned in modern times, because if there is some doubt about the ability to play the full game the match is more likely to be postponed.

However, the Middlesbrough *v.* Oldham Athletic Division One game on 3 April 1915 was abandoned after 55 minutes when Athletic's full-back, Billy Cook refused to accept the referee's decision to dismiss him.

The Latics had gone to Ayresome Park needing a win to effectively secure the League Championship. When Cook was sent off, Oldham were 4–1 down and, as he refused to leave the field, the referee abandoned the game.

Accrington Stanley

Accrington Stanley joined the Football League as founder members of the Third Division (North) in 1921–22.

The two clubs first met in the 1935–36 season, Latics winning 3–0 at Boundary Park, though Accrington gained revenge by scoring the only goal of the game at Peel Park. Accrington only completed the 'double' over the Latics on one occasion and that was in season 1954–55, whilst Oldham did the 'double' on six occasions.

The two clubs last met in 1960–61 and the two games could not have been more of a contrast. Accrington won their home game 5–1, whilst Latics triumphed 5–2 in the return, with Bert Lister scoring a hat-trick. After spending a total of thirty-three full seasons in the League, a financial crisis forced them to withdraw from the League on 6 March 1962 and their record was expunged.

 Bobby Collins—he was in his 43rd year when he made his last appearance at Boundary Park on 20 April 1973.

Age

Youngest: The youngest player to appear in a Football League fixture for Oldham Athletic FC was Eddie Hopkinson who made his league debut match against Crewe Alexandra (Home 1–3) on 12 January 1952, when he was 16 years 75 days.

Oldest: The oldest player to line-up in a Latics' first team in the Football League was Bobby Collins. He was 42 years 63 days when he last turned out for the club in a goal-less draw at home to Rochdale on 20 April 1973.

Aldershot

In March 1992, the Liquidator called in to supervise the winding-up of the 'Shots', confirming to the Football League that no offers had been received for the Fourth Division club.

Latics met Aldershot for the first time on 6 September 1958 in the Fourth Division, going down 0–1 at Boundary Park. Though they won the return at the Recreation Ground 3–1, they failed to score in the next four encounters as Aldershot completed the 'double' in seasons 1959–60 and 1960–61.

The next five matches at Boundary Park were all won by Latics and in the 5–2 victory on 22 September 1970 David Shaw scored the only hat-trick in a match between these two sides.

Appearances

The players with the highest number of appearances for Oldham Athletic FC are as follows:

	Football League	FA and Football League Cups	Total
Ian Wood	517 (7)	45 (1)	562 (8)
Roger Palmer	421 (47)	44 (5)	465 (52)
David Wilson	368	29	397
Ronnie Blair	369 (12)	31 (2)	390 (14)
Howard Matthews	344	24	368
Jim Bowie	331 (3)	30 (1)	361 (4)
Jimmy Frizzell	309 (9)	33	342 (9)
Maurice Whittle	307 (5)	31	338 (5)
Matthew Gray	290	11	301
Les Adlam	279	11	290

Consecutive Appearances

Only David Wilson and Jimmy Fay made over one hundred consecutive League appearances immediately following their debut for the club in that competition.

David Wilson: 170 appearances
  Debut 9 September 1907 v. Stoke City (Away) 3–1

Jimmy Fay: 152 appearances
  Debut 9 September 1907 v. Stoke City (Away) 3–1

Five players have made over one hundred consecutive appearances at any time during their careers with Oldham Athletic.

Teddy Ivill: 224 appearances
  From 30 April 1927 to 29 October 1932

Ian Wood: 147 appearances
  From 16 March 1971 to 27 April 1974

Maurice Whittle : 144 appearances
  From 23 October 1971 to 7 December 1974

Earl Barratt: 135 appearances
  From 11 March 1989 to 15 February 1992

Roger Palmer: 112 appearances
From 26 December 1981 to 18 September 1984

Artificial Pitch

There was a major development at Boundary Park in the summer of 1986 – the installation of an artificial pitch. For with the help of grants and the backing of Oldham Council, it was to provide consistent year-round training and playing facilities not only for the club, but also for the general public.

It was a race against time for the contractors to complete the installation in readiness for the first home game against Barnsley on 25 August, which Latics won 2–0, and were surprised to learn that the plastic needed watering to help it bed in.

David Ashworth

David Ashworth's appointment as the club's first manager, coincided with Athletic's return to Boundary Park from Hudson Fold in 1906. A first-class referee from Waterford, he was said to be only about five feet in height and therefore must have been one of the smallest managers ever. Within four years of him taking charge, he had guided the team from the Lancashire Combination to the First Division of the Football League. David Ashworth was usually seen sporting a bowler hat with a waxed moustache. His rather stern appearance obviously disguised a strong sense of humour, for he was said to wear his 'tash with both ends upturned after a win, both ends down after a defeat, and one up and one down after a draw.'

During the close season of 1914, David Ashworth resigned to join Stockport County. He took over as Liverpool manager in December 1919 and after twice finishing in fourth place, he took them to the First Division championship in 1921–22. He was well on course for a second successive League championship with Liverpool when the Athletic's

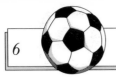
directors persuaded him to return to Boundary Park to see if his old magic could stem the club's downward slide. It was unfortunately "too late" to save the side from its first-ever relegation.

After just one season in the Second Division, he left for Manchester City, where he stayed for 16 months.

Subsequent appointments included spells as manager at Walsall, Caernarvon and Llanelly and scout for Blackpool.

Affectionately known as 'Little Dave' he died at Blackpool on 23 March 1947, aged 79 years.

Oldham's full league record under David Ashworth was:

P	W	D	L	F	A
327	140	83	104	480	392

Attendances at

Boundary Park

Opponents	Date	Competition	Attendance
Individual matches: highest in the Football League			
Blackpool	21 April 1930	Division 2	45,120
Hull City	26 April 1949	Division 3 (North)	35,200
Bolton Wanderers	10 April 1909	Division 2	35,000
Newcastle United	10 September 1910	Division 1	34,000
Stockport County	8 March 1952	Division 3 (North)	33,450
Bolton Wanderers	26 December 1921	Division 1	32,814
Newcastle United	25 December 1911	Division 1	32,000
Tottenham Hotspur	17 April 1922	Division 1	31,343
Blackburn Rovers	26 September 1953	Division 2	30,832
Everton	29 April 1954	Division 2	30,072

Lowest attendances in the Football League

Northampton Town	29 April 1969	Division 3	2,073
Walsall	29 December 1968	Division 3	2,086
Bristol Rovers	11 May 1968	Division 3	2,089
Walsall	12 April 1960	Division 4	2,264
Reading	18 February 1969	Division 3	2,297
Lincoln City	10 February 1970	Division 4	2,391

Other games at Boundary Park

Sheffield Wednesday	25 January 1930	FA Cup Round 4	46,471
Sheffield Wednesday	27 January 1934	FA Cup Round 4	46,011
Liverpool	27 January 1962	FA Cup Round 4	41,733
Everton	24 February 1912	FA Cup Round 3	35,473
Wolverhampton Wanderers	11 January 1930	FA Cup Round 3	32,355
Newcastle United	7 January 1950	FA Cup Round 3	31,706
Huddersfield Town	9 January 1932	FA Cup Round 3	30,607
Cardiff City	8 January 1949	FA Cup Round 3	28,991
Bristol Rovers	10 January 1962	FA Cup Round 3 (Rep)	27,063
Manchester United	22 February 1913	FA Cup Round 3	26,932

Oldham Athletic's average home attendances over the last ten years have been as follows:

1984–85	4,471	1989–90	9,727
1985–86	4,651	1990–91	13.247
1986–87	6,883	1991–92	15,087
1987–88	6,906	1992–93	12,859
1988–89	7,204	1993–94	12,440

Away

Opponents	Date	Competition	Score
	Best away wins		
27 September 1947	Darlington	Division 3 (North)	6–0
19 October 1935	Rochdale	Division 3 (North)	6–2
12 December 1925	Stockton	FA Cup Round 4	6–4
3 September 1952	Darlington	Division 3 (North)	5–0
30 December 1961	Southport	Division 4	5–0
	Worst away defeats		
26 December 1935	Tranmere Rovers	Division 3 (North)	4–13
5 April 1958	Hull City	Division 3 (North)	0–9
26 May 1947	Rotherham United	Division 3 (North)	0–8
19 December 1953	Hull City	Division 2	0–8
27 February 1960	Northampton Town	Division 4	1–8
26 November 1969	Peterborough United	Division 4	1–8
6 March 1954	Rotherham United	Division 2	0–7
26 December 1912	Aston Villa	Division 1	1–7
22 March 1913	Blackburn Rovers	Division 1	1–7
27 November 1920	Burnley	Division 1	1–7
24 September 1962	Sunderland	Football League Cup Round 2	1–7
	Highest scoring away draws		
13 February 1937	Rotherham United	Division 3 (North)	4–4
19 August 1953	Luton Town	Division 2	4–4
3 September 1955	Rochdale	Division 3 (North)	4–4
30 March 1957	Wrexham	Division 3 (North)	4–4
2 November 1957	Mansfield Town	Division 3 (North)	4–4
26 November 1960	Chesterfield	FA Cup Round 2	4–4

Most Away Wins in a Season: 12 in 1973–74 (Division 3)

Least Away Wins in a Season: 0 in 1934–35 (Division 2)

0 in 1974–75 (Divison 2)

Most Away Defeats in a Season: 18 in 1934–35 (Divison 2)

18 in 1958–59 (Division 4)

Least Away Defeats in a Season: 5 in 1952–53 (Division 3 N.)

5 in 1973–74 (Division 3)

Most Away Goals in a Season: 38 in 1947–48 (Division 3 N.)

Least Away Goals in a Season: 11 in 1924–25 (Division 2)

Herbert Bamlett

Latics' second manager had, like David Ashworth, been a referee and signed off at the top of refereeing circles, his last match in charge being the FA Cup final of 1914 between Burnley and Liverpool. This was the last Cup Final to be held at Crystal Palace and the first to be honoured by the presence of the reigning monarch, King George V.

Taking over the reins at Boundary Park in June 1914, Bamlett inherited a fine Oldham side in the season which kicked off with World War One already a month old.

The Latics enjoyed their best ever season, finishing First Division runners-up in 1914–15.

Called up for military service in the summer of 1916, Herbert Bamlett faced the difficult task of reconstructing the team following his demobilization in February 1919.

Losing players of the calibre of Charlie Roberts, Joe Donnachie and Oliver Tummon, who were difficult to replace, the club turned in two seasons of indifferent performances. In May 1921, Bamlett resigned his position to take charge of Wigan Borough's first season in the new Third Division North.

In 1923 he joined Middlesbrough and from the summer of 1927 to April 1931, he was Manchester United's manager. His last season at

Old Trafford saw the Reds concede 115 goals and finish bottom of the First Division.

Oldham's full league record under Herbert Bamlett was:

P	W	D	L	F	A
122	41	34	47	168	194

Best Starts

Oldham's best start to a Football League season came in 1990–91 when the club were unbeaten for the first sixteen games of that campaign. Starting the season with a 3–2 win at Wolverhampton, courtesy of an Ian Marshall hat-trick, the Latics went on to win their first five games to record the following best start:

P	W	D	L	F	A
16	11	5	0	32	15

The Latics continued this good form throughout the remainder of the season to win the Division Two Championship.

Billy Pot

Latics first manager, David Ashworth, always watched the matches from the Flat Stand, Broadway side, running up and down with his 'Billy Pot' on his head, keeping up with play.

During a game with Leeds City on 19 December 1908, which Oldham won 6–0, he was running down with F. Hesham and nearly ran off the end of the stand, ending in an undignified sitting position.

Blackburn Rovers

The Latics and Blackburn Rovers created a piece of Football League history on Boxing Day 1981. Their Second Division fixture was switched from Ewood Park to Boundary Park after it became obvious that the Rovers ground could not be saved from the big freeze.

Although many FA Cup ties had been switched in the past, it was the first time that a Football League fixture had been reversed. Blackburn won the match 3–0 in front of 15,400 spectators, whilst gate receipts of just under £24,000 produced a new club record.

It was also Blackburn Rovers in the previous season who provided Oldham with their 1000th victory in the Football League. Their 1–0 win at Boundary Park on 11 November 1980 came courtesy of a Jim Steel goal.

Ronnie Blair—a Northern Ireland International and one of Latics' most versatile and accomplished players.

Ronnie Blair

Ronnie Blair spent two spells at Boundary Park, initially joining the club from Coleraine in July 1966. He made his league debut for the Latics against Shrewsbury in

January 1967, but three years later and after a short loan spell with Preston North End, he was transferred to Rochdale. The first spell had seen him play in 78 league matches for the Latics, scoring just two goals.

In August 1972 he returned to Oldham, and in 1973–74 when the club won the Third Division championship he had a most successful season, scoring 11 goals from 41 appearances.

In October 1974, he was given his International debut for Northern Ireland against Sweden in Solna. Ronnie went on to win five full caps for his country, playing his last game in 1976 against Israel.

One of Oldham's most versatile and accomplished players, he could play in all defensive positions and in midfield. He combined dash, determination and good constructive ideas in both of his roles.

In 1980–81, his final season at the club, he was the only ever-present in Latics' Division Two campaign.

A fine professional and a great favourite during his two spells at Boundary Park, he left the club to sign for Blackpool. He had made 371 League appearances for the Latics and scored 23 goals.

Boundary Park

Originally home of Oldham County, the first sod had been ceremonially cut in July 1896 with a silver spade now kept in Oldham's VIP suite. The first match should have been played on 19 September 1896 when Robert Ascroft MP kicked off a friendly *v.* Chorley, but the weather was so appalling that both he and the teams had to seek refuge in the dressing rooms and the game was abandoned. When the Latics returned to the ground a second time, their inaugural match was on 1 September 1906 *v.* Colne.

Boundary Park had two stands in its early days. On the site of the present Main Stand stood a quite substantial pitch-roofed stand with covered seats and an open paddock.

Opposite was the Flat or Broadway Stand, built hastily when Oldham were elected to the Football League in 1907.

While early photographs show how spectators stood on top of the flat roof, Oldham's manager, the bowler-hatted David Ashworth, went

Boundary Park, with the new Rochdale Road End Stand.

further by running along the roof in order to follow play. The present Main Stand was begun in 1913 but not completed until 1920.

The Latics were already an average Second Divison team when in October 1927 the Chadderton Road Stand, a covered terrace, was opened. But not for long. A winter's gale blew it down again soon after.

Boundary Park's highest ever attendance 47,671 came to watch Athletic's Fourth Round FA Cup tie *v.* Sheffield Wednesday, the First Division Champions on 25 January 1930.

Three decades later the club had to seek re-election and was, in fact, near to closing down completely, but a year later the Latics installed new floodlights, first switched on for a friendly *v.* Burnley on 3 October 1961—they were the last Lancashire League club to have lights. In 1971 a new stand was built, for Oldham not only won promotion but also a short-lived competition known as the Ford Sporting League.

Held for one season only, Ford gave points for goals, but deducted them for bad behaviour on the pitch. They stipulated that the club had

to spend their £70,000 prize money on ground improvements. The result was a quickly-built new stand named after the sponsor, in place of the old Broadway Stand.

Being one of the highest grounds in Britain, Oldham's pitch was prone to freezing, so in 1980 undersoil heating at a cost of £60,000 was installed. This meant the pitch was usable when most of the Latics' neighbours were out of action. For example, Oldham Rugby League Club played a match there, and on Boxing Day 1981, the authorities allowed the Blackburn Rovers *v.* Latics match due to be played at Ewood Park to be switched to Boundary Park.

The chances of Oldham staging most matches in all weathers was increased in 1986 when Boundary Park became the fourth league ground to install artificial turf.

Plans to move Oldham fans to the Rochdale Road End have been delayed because of extra and additional turnstiles needed from the car park area. But the Latics are going ahead with the re-roofing of the George Hill main stand.

The new cover will be brought further forward to cover 700 new seats in the paddocks and will be translucent. This will help sunshine penetrate the edge of the pitch trapped in frost while the rest has cleared!

Jim Bowie

Jim Bowie was playing Scottish junior football for Arthurlie Juniors when he was recommended to Oldham. A clever ball-playing inside-forward or half-back, Jim was groomed as the successor to Bobby Johnstone and made his league debut for the club in the goal-less draw at Newport County on 20 August 1962.

He scored his first goal for the club in the return fixture nine days later, hitting the winners as Latics won 3–2.

Throughout his ten-year stay at Boundary Park, "Big Jim" Bowie became a firm favourite with Oldham fans.

Always cool under pressure and with an elegant style, he always tried to use the ball to good advantage. Standing 6ft 2ins, his height ensured that he won most aerial encounters.

In his first season with the club he made 14 league appearances and scored five goals, four of these coming in successive matches. Not a prolific goal-scorer, he netted on 38 occasions during his 334 league appearances for the club. It is no co-incidence to say that his only ever-present season, 1970–71, was the one when the Latics won the Ford Sporting League.

Jim Bowie—a firm favourite with the Boundary Park crowd.

Bradford Park Avenue

Park Avenue enjoyed 47 seasons in the League before failing to hold on to their place in 1969–70 after three consecutive seasons at the bottom of the League.

They started their career in the Second Division in 1908–9. The clubs first met at Bradford on 15 December 1908, with Latics winning 4–3. In fact, Oldham completed the 'double' that season, winning the return at Boundary Park 2–0. The following season, the Latics needed a Jimmy Fay penalty to rescue a home point, but triumphed 6–1 at Park Avenue! In 1914–15, Park Avenue joined their Bradford neighbours,

City, in the first Division. Visiting Boundary Park that season, they were well beaten 6–2 with Gilbert Kemp grabbing a hat-trick.

The Bradford club were relegated in 1920–21 and the following season suffered the embarrassment of dropping into the Third Division (North). They returned to the Second Division in 1928 and it was not until 1950–51 that they were next relegated.

Latics dropped into the Third Division (North) at the end of the 1934–35 season and did not meet with Park Avenue until 1950–51, when the Bradford side completed the 'double' over the Boundary Park outfit.

Founder members of the Fourth Division, they won promotion just once before their eventual demise at the end of the 1969–70 season—a season which saw Latics play out two goal-less draws with their Yorkshire opponents.

Brothers

Garry Hoolickin.

There have been five sets of brothers that have played for the Latics. Dan and Bill Hooper were the nephews of Charlie Roberts, the Athletic centre-forward, and played for Latics in the first season of peacetime football 1919–20.

A tall, well-built centre-forward, Don Travis confounded his critics with 32 goals in his first season of his second spell with the club, for in his initial spell at Boundary Park he failed to make an

Steve Hoolickin. He was a talented defender who was unfortunate to be in the shadow of Ian Wood, whilst Gary was a versatile defender who made over 200 appearances in the Latics first team.

impression. His elder brother Harry Travis played for Athletic during the war.

Bill Naylor was signed from Huddersfield Town shortly after his demobilization from the Fleet Air Arm. He had a remarkable period of service with Athletic, qualifying for two benefits. His younger brother Harold Naylor made only one appearance in the Latics first-team as a late replacement for Eric Gemmell.

Steve Hoolickin was unfortunate to be in the shadow of Latics' full-back Ian Wood, whilst Gary Hoolickin, a versatile defender, went on to make over 200 league appearances for the club.

Twin-brothers Paul and Ron Futcher played for Oldham in the eighties. A cool and competent defender, Paul Futcher's self-assurance and skill made him one of the best defenders in the Second Division, whilst Ron Futcher's clever footballing brain paid dividends when this splended short-term acquisition averaged a goal every other game for Athletic, including ten goals in the first ten matches of 1986–87.

Captains

Joe Stafford was the only survivor of the club's Pine Villa days to play for Athletic in a Football League fixture. As club captain he was without doubt the driving force behind their early successes in junior football and in the Lancashire Combination.

On his arrival at Boundary Park and after 172 league appearances for Manchester United, Alex Downie was elected captian. His leadership and general influence did much to ensure Latics' promotion to Division One as runners-up to Manchester City in 1909–10.

It was under Charlie Roberts' captaincy that Athletic achieved their best ever league position, when they ended the 1914–15 season one point behind Everton, the League Champions. A great captain, he was almost unbeatable in the air and cost Athletic a club record fee when he joined them from Manchester United.

A popular and inspiring captain, Beau Ratcliffe missed only nine games in four seasons as he kept Athletic on the verge of promotion. The club finishing 7th, 4th, 4th and 5th in his four seasons as captain.

George Hardwick was a born leader who skippered every team for which he played, which included leading Latics to the Third Divison North Championship in 1952–53. Archie Whyte had refused the captaincy at this time, because he was superstitious and liked to be last on to the pitch!

Bill Cranston was signed by Jimmy Frizzell who made him captain. The outstanding defender responded by helping the Latics to promotion from Divison Four in his first season at Boundary Park.

Centre of Excellence

The setting up of a Football Association—approved Centre of Excellence for boys aged 12 and over was a significant development for Oldham's long-term future.

Under the guidance of qualified coaches, including Latics' Willie
Donachie and Billy Urmson, it replaced the club's "Search for a Star"
scheme, which in its first year produced local lad Mike Flynn.

Centuries

There are only two instances of individual players who have scored 100
or more goals for the Latics. Roger Palmer is the greatest goalscorer
with 141 strikes in his Oldham career (1980–1994) while Eric Gemmell
scored 109 goals between 1947 and 1954.

Only David Wilson (170) and Jimmy Fay (152) have made over a
hundred consecutive appearances immediately after making their
Football League debuts.

Chairmen

On 29 October 1948, veteran director and former chairman Arthur
Barlow, stated that he was prepared to lend the club, free of interest,
£2,000 for an unspecified period, on condition that 15 other supporters
each make an equal loan. This was his challenge to the Oldham Athletic
shareholders who were urging swift action to sign the Middlesbrough
and England player, Wilt Mannion. The Ayresome Park outfit were
willing to transfer him for £25,000, but the arrangement never mate-
rialised and the deal fell through.

In 1962, Athletic's chairman Harry Massey offered the Oldham
players a £5 per goal bonus prior to the game against Southport at
Boundary Park on Boxing Day. The Latics won the game by 11–0, Mr
Massey paid out, but withdrew his offer for subsequent matches!

Championships

The first championship that the Latics won was the Third Division (North) in 1952–53.

The championship was in doubt right up to the last match of the season. A 0–0 draw at Valley Parade ensured that the Latics finished a point ahead of Port Vale.

Latics won the Third Division championship in 1973–74. Wearing all-blue for most of the season, they sealed their successful season with a 0–0 draw at Plymouth. It was a great campaign, punctuated with some brilliant team and individual performances, but it was the side's remarkable consistency over a ten match, twenty point run from January 12 to March 12, which made it all possible.

The Latics won the Second Divison championship in 1990–91, after a series of near misses in both League and Cup competitions.

They started the season with five straight wins and were undefeated until the 17th game of the campaign. Seven defeats in 44 League games underlined the Latics consistency—it was the first trophy in management for Joe Royle, now the longest serving manager in the Football League.

The final game of the season saw Neil Redfearn slot home a 90th minute penalty as the Latics beat Sheffield Wednesday 3–2 in front of the club's best home league attendance of 18,809 to clinch the title.

Clean Sheet

This is the colloquial expression to describe a goalkeeper's performance when he does not concede a goal.

In the Football League, three Oldham goalkeepers have kept 16 clean sheets in a season. In 1938–39, Lewis Caunce became the first to achieve this feat, obviously managing to put behind him the memory of Boxing Day 1935, when Tranmere Rovers put 13 goals past him on his fourth appearance in Athletic's goal!

Signed as cover for Fred Ogden, George Burnett equalled the feat from 42 appearances in the championship campaign of 1952–53. The latest

Latics goalkeeper to equal the feat was Andy Goram in season 1986–87, when the club reached the play-offs. In fact, Andy didn't concede a goal in the first six matches of the season, but came down to earth with a bump in the seventh match as Huddersfield Town beat the Latics 5–4!

Colours

As Pine Villa, the club wore red and white stripes and in their first game as the new Oldham Athletic Association Club.

From 1910–1966 the club wore shirts with broad blue and white bands, though in 1946–47, the club wore red and white hooped rugby shirts on loan.

From 1967–1972 the Latics sported shirts of tangerine and blue, whilst from 1972 to the present day the club have worn all blue with slight variations.

Consecutive Home Games

The Latics were involved in an intense sequence of six home games in succession in the 1946–47 season. After playing away at Tranmere on 16 November 1946 and losing 2–4, Latics were involved in the following list of matches at Boundary Park, before visiting New Brighton on Boxing Day, where they lost 0–4.

Date	Opponents	Competition	Score
23 November	Darlington	Division 3 (North)	2–0
30 November	Tranmere Rovers	FA Cup Round 1	1–0
7 December	Gateshead	Division 3 (North)	1–1
14 Decmeber	Doncaster Rovers	FA Cup Round 2	1–2
21 December	Crewe Alexandra	Division 3 (North)	3–1
25 December	New Brighton	Division 3 (North)	2–2
10 March	Liverpool	Division One	2–1

Cricketers

The only Latics player who was a cricketer of real note was Billy Cook. Suspended for 12 months from 16 April 1915 he was a fine all-round cricketer, playing for Lancashire from 1905–07. In 11 matches for the county, he scored 307 runs at 21.92 and took 51 wickets at 18.54, including 7 for 64 against Gloucestershire on his debut. Later he was professional with Royton, Burnley, Colne and Rawtenstall.

Local club, Crompton attracted a number of Latics' players into their side. One of the first was Tom Smelt who, though he only played twice for Oldham's first team, was Crompton's professional in 1930. Not only did Harry Jackson open the batting for Crompton, but he represented the Lancashire Second XI. After scoring eight goals for the 'A' team against Preston North End 'A', he followed it up a week later by scoring five for the Reserves against Southport Reserves. Given a rare first-team outing, he failed to score and was dropped!

Other talented batsmen include Tommy Bell and Billy Dearden, whose career blossomed fully after his Oldham days when he scored goals in all four divisions of the Football League.

Other league cricketers included Bill Lawton, the husband of the popular stage, screen and radio acress Dora Bryan. The Latics' attacking wing-half was probably better known as a cricketer, serving Werneth, Ashton, Eccleshill, St Anne's, Whitehaven and Walsall before returning to Oldham in 1957. Speedy winger Ernest Steele made a lot of runs for Middleton in the Central Lancashire League after playing as a professional with Farsley in the Bradford League and representing Lancashire Second XI on a number of occasions.

George Milligan played for Woodhouses and was awarded the 'Ashton Reporter' bat for hitting 320 runs in four consecutive innings, whilst Colin Whitaker played Minor Counties cricket for Shropshire.

Crowd Trouble

However unwelcome, crowd disturbances are far from a modern phenomenon at major football matches. Behaviour at Boundary Park has usually been of a high standard and though Latics supporters are well-renowed for voicing their opinions at suspect referees, the occasions when their demonstrations boil over beyond the verbal are very rare indeed.

Perhaps the most noticeable of these occasions was the match against Sheffield Wednesday on 6 September 1980. It was marred by a crowd disturbance which forced the game to be held up for 29 minutes, as a minority element among Sheffield supporters got onto the pitch.

The incident was sparked off by the dismissal of Wednesday's flying winger Terry Curran for kicking Latics' Simon Stainrod as the referee was booking both players.

Nine days later, Football's top officials came to Oldham to hold an inquiry into the "riots" and came to the conclusion after seven hours of talks that the Latics should be exonerated of all blame.

The FA Commission decided that the ground and safety improvements at Boundary Park were more than adequate and that the blame must lay with Sheffield Wednesday as being responsible for the actions of their supporters. Oldham won the match 2–0 to record their 999th victory in the Football League.

Death

Former Oldham full-back Sam Wynne became the first player to die in a first-class fixture when on Saturday 30 April 1927, he collapsed after 40 minutes of the Bury *v.* Sheffield United Division One match while taking a free-kick.

He died in the dressing room and a post-mortem showed that he had been suffering from pneumonia. The game was abandoned and replayed the following Thursday with all the receipts going to Sam Wynne's widow. Making five appearances in the Athletic first team,

George Joynson's death at the age of 24 in July 1914 was a direct result of sunstroke sustained during a heat-wave. In both of his seasons at Boundary Park he was the leading scorer for the Reserves. His performance in 1913–14 included nine goals in eight days around Christmas.

Debuts

One of the club's oldest debutants was George Bradshaw who was 37 years 5 months when he played in goal, for the one and only time, in a 5–4 defeat at home to Rotherham in the opening game of the 1950–51 season. Yet Jack Warner played his first game for Oldham only a month before his 40th birthday in a goal-less draw at Southport on 18 August 1951.

Dave Pearson was signed by manager Ted Goodier from Darwen and became one of the few players to mark his league debut (at home to Halifax on 21 August 1956) with a hat-trick. Arthur Ormston was another Oldham centre-forward. He scored a treble on his debut at home to Fulham in September 1925. In fact within the space of two days he had scored eight goals, as he hit five in Oldham's 7–2 win over Stoke City. Maurice Wellock too made a sensation debut for Latics, scoring four goals in the club's 5–2 win at Grimsby on 12 February 1927, yet he remained at Boundary Park for only three months, as Latics tried six centre-forwards during that campaign.

John Collins burst onto the Boundary Park scene with six goals in a floodlit friendly match against FC Thun of Switzerland. His transfer included the payment of an additional £75 for every goal he scored, but after a few weeks this was dispensed with and he returned to Queen's Park Rangers.

Len Dickinson made a stunning debut for Athletic's Reserve side in the match against Lytham on 19 August 1961. He scored five goals, including a hat-trick in seven minutes. On his debut for the first-team, 'Little Len' as he was known netted as last-gasp equaliser at Exeter.

Charles Hemseley scored on his debut in the match against Manchester United at Old Trafford, but unfortunately the game was

abandoned through fog with 15 minutes still remaining and Latics still ahead.

Perhaps the saddest debut by any Latics player was that of Arden Maddison at Maine Road on 1 October 1927. He caused a great sensation when he was sent-off in an ill-tempered derby game against Manchester City.

Defeats

Individual Games

Oldham's worst *home* defeat in a first-class match was the 2–7 scoreline inflicted on the club by Newcastle United on 7 January 1950 in the Third Round of the FA Cup.

Away from home, the club's heaviest defeat was the 13–4 defeat by Tranmere Rovers on Boxing Day 1935.

Over a Single Season

Latics' worst defensive record in terms of defeats suffered in a single season was in 1934–35, when the club lost 26 out of 42 Second Division matches and were relegated. The club also lost 26 matches in their first two seasons in the Fourth Division (1958–59 and 1959–60) though this was from a 46 match programme.

Conversely, the Latics' only lost eight matches in both 1909–10 and 1990–91 when gaining promotion to the First Division.

Consecutive League Matches without defeat

Oldham's best run of league games without defeat is 15 and was established in 1937–38. The run began on 25 September 1937 with a 3–1 home win over Hartlepool United and finished with a goal-less draw at home to Crewe Alexandra on 15 January 1938.

Defensive Records

Oldham Athletic's *best* defensive record in the Football League was established in 1909–10 when the club won promotion from Division Two. The Latics conceded 39 goals in that campaign and were beaten in only eight matches.

The club's *worst* defensive record in the Football League was in 1934–35 when they let in 95 goals in 42 matches and were relegated to Division Three (North) for the first time in their history.

Dismissals

Although sendings-off are an all too common feature of the modern game, no-one should think that football has ever been immune from them.

When Latics visited Middlesbrough on 3 April 1915, the referee sent off Billy Cook, but the bald Oldham full-back refused to leave the field. The game was abandoned and Cook was suspended for 12 months.

When Arden Maddison made his football league debut against Manchester City on 1 October 1927, he caused a sensation when he was sent-off during an ill-tempered derby match.

Norman Dodgin

One of the game's youngest managers, Norman Dodgin's playing career began with Newcastle United in August 1940. After serving in the Forces he returned to St James' Park and in 1947–48 made 26 appearances as the Magpies won promotion to Division One. After transferring first to Reading and then Northampton, he took his first step into management with Exeter City in August 1953, at a time when

he had yet to reach his 32nd birthday. Following spells with Yeovil Town and Barrow, he arrived at Boundary Park in July 1958 with a reputation for catching players young and moulding them himself. The youngsters were inevitably thrown into a struggling Oldham side. The team's results reflecting the problems that successive applications for re-election had brought.

Norman Dodgin's last game as Oldham manager was the final fixture of the 1959–60 season at home to Notts County. The programme was usually printed in blue, but mistakenly (though not inappropriately) it was printed in black! The visitors won the game 3–0 to secure promotion as runners-up. On leaving Boundary Park, he took over a large newsagent's business in Exeter.

Oldham's full league record under Norman Dodgin was:

P	W	D	L	F	A
92	24	16	52	100	167

Draws

Oldham played their greatest number of drawn League matches in a single season (21) in 1988–89 when they finished sixteenth in the Second Division, to equal that Division's highest total of draws in a season, set by Leeds United in 1982–83. Their fewest number of drawn League matches was 4 in 1958–59, the club's first-ever season in the Fourth Division.

The Latics also share the Third Division (North) record for the highest number of draws. For in 1955–56, the club drew 18 of their 46 matches to equal the record held by Wrexham (1923–24) Scunthorpe United (1950–51) Port Vale (1952–53) and Bradford city (1952–53).

The club's highest scoring draw is 4–4, a scoreline in eight Latics' matches—Gateshead (Home 1936–37) Rotherham United (Away 1936–37) Luton Town (Away 1953–54) Rochdale (Away 1955–56) Wrexham (Away 1956–57) Mansfield Town (Away 1957–58) Chesterfield (Away 1960–61) and Bolton Wanderers (Home 1984–85) though

this latter scoreline in the League Cup was after extra-time and saw the Trotters go through.

The club as Pine Villa did draw 5–5 away to Larkhill in the opening match of the 1898–99 season, whilst a similar scoreline was played out at home to Bury in the First Competition of the League's northern section in 1941–42.

The greatest number of drawn matches in a single Oldham cup-tie is two. This has happened on three occasions on the FA Cup—Crewe Alexandra (1949–50) Cambridge United (1973–74) and Everton (1989–90) and twice in the Football League Cup—Workington (1967–68) and Brighton and Hove Albion (1977–78).

Election Campaigns

David Ashworth, a referee from Waterford, became the club's first manager in 1906 and with the results in the Lancashire Combination going well, there began a determined campaign to get the Latics in the Football League.

Every town now visited by Oldham supporters began to boast stickers declaring "Oldham wants League football".

Success seemed certain for Athletic as the clubs canvassed all the League clubs, securing votes for their annual election. However, on the day of the voting, Oldham missed election by just one vote!

Undeterred, the club embarked on the 1906–7 season in the Combination in high spirits. It was in that season that the half-back line of Fay, Walders and Wilson emerged and if they couldn't succeed in winning votes, then Athletic could succeed at football.

During that season, the Latics won the Combination Championship and reached the second round proper of the FA Cup. Yet surprisingly, despite all their success, the Latics won fewer votes than the previous year at the Football League election.

Resigned to spending another season in the Combination, the club suddenly found that their dreams of League soccer turned into reality, as Burslem Port Vale were forced to resign from the Second Division because of financial troubles.

Electronic Scoreboard

The electronic scoreboard at Boundary Park was built to withstand the strongest gales that the Pennines could offer, but blew down in the first easterly wind of the 1989–90 season!

However, it was to take centre stage on many a memorable day as the Latics' cup exploits became legendary.

Towards the end of that successful season, Joe Royle declined the chance to talk to Manchester City about their vacant managerial post. It was the depth of feeling among Latics fans that persuaded him to stay. Supporters paid for messages on the electronic scoreboard reading—"Please Joe, Don't Go".

Ever Presents

There have been 46 Oldham Athletic players who have been ever-present throughout a Football League season. The greatest number of ever-present seasons by a Latics player is 7, the record being held by David Wilson.

The full list is:

No. of Seasons	Players
7	D. Wilson
5	E. Ivill
4	J. Fay
3	E. Barrett, J. Naylor, R. Palmer, M. Whittle, I. Wood
2	L. Chapman, S. King, W. Porter, M. Ward

No. of Seasons	Players
1	L. Adlam, P. Atkinson, A. Barlow, T. Bell, D. Best, R. Blair, J. Bowie, K. Branagan, L. Caunce, J. Colquhoun, R. Freeman, M. Gray, J. Hallworth, N. Henry, K. Hicks, R. Holden, L Horton, R. Ledger, P. McCall, H. McDonald, P. McDonnell, G. McVitie, M. Milligan, C. Ogden, W. Pickering, C. Roberts, F. Scholfield, T. Seymour, G. Sharp, I. Towers, O. Tummon, T. Walker, A. Whyte, A. Williams

Father and Son

There have been six father and son combinations that have represented the Latics.

Tommy Bell and his son Graham both made 170 league appearances for Oldham Athletic. Tommy was an excellent defender, who tackled hard and used the ball constructively, whilst Graham ran the Oldham midfield with a flair and enthusiasm that attracted the then England manager Don Revie.

Fred and Chris Ogden were both goalkeepers. Quick and agile on his feet, Fred Ogden became the regular first-team goalkeeper from the middle of the 1948–49 season until September 1951 when he fractured a collar bone. His son Chris had a torrid time in his first spell of League football, conceding 16 goals in his first six matches. But by the following season his confidence had grown, and he too became a first-team regular.

Tommy Wright senior was a versatile forward who won three Scottish caps in his days at Roker Park. His son Tommy Wright junior joined Oldham from Leeds United in October 1986 for a fee of £80,000. Used by the Latics as a wide attacker, his scampering runs down the left wing unsettled many defences.

After a long and distinguished career at Maine Road, Ken Branagan was for six seasons the most conspicuous figure in the Latics' defence. His son Jim Branagan was the Reserve team captain and a splendid deputy for regular full-backs, Wood and Whittle. A consistent member

of the Blackburn Rovers team, he made 294 league appearances for the Ewood Park club.

A firm favourite with the Boundary Park crowd, Alan Williams was without doubt the Latics best centre-half of the 1960s. His son Gary was recommended to Latics manager Joe Royle by former Bristol City colleagues Chris Garland and Geoff Merrick. A well-balanced midfield player, he made 45 appearances at league level for the club.

George Jones arrived at Boundary Park as a replacement for David Shaw. Though he quickly proved his ability, it was at Bury where he scored a century of goals in two spells that he made his name. His son Alex started his career with Oldham, but was released on a free-transfer at the end of 1985–86. Joining Preston, he was the only ever-present in North End's fine promotion side of the following season.

Jimmy Fay

Jimmy Fay was an outstanding member of the legendary middle line of Fay, Walders and Wilson, who between them played no small part in lifting the Latics from obscurity into the First Division of the Football League. Born in Southport, he began his career with local sides Blue Star and Southport Working Lads. He turned professional in 1903 after joining Chorley and subsequently played for Oswald-twistle Rovers.

When Jimmy Fay came to see the Oldham officials to sign, they offered him 2s 6d, less wage than he wanted. After the officials had refused to alter their decision, he walked out of the public house where the meeting was being held.

One of the officials, who had seen Fay play, told the club that not only had they lost a good half-back, but also a good inside-forward. The official was then told to go after him and sign him. This he did, Fay signing at the entrance to Werneth Station.

His first appearance for Oldham Athletic was at Hudson Fold in season 1905–06 against Atherton Church in the Lancashire Combination 'A' Division. Between 1907–08 and 1910–11, he did not miss a League game for Oldham and was the club's leading scorer in 1909–10 with 26 goals from inside-forward. Moved out of defence to bolster the attack, he scored 21 goals in 26 matches, including a hat-trick in a 5–0 home win over Barnsley.

A tailor's shop in Yorkshire Street offered an overcoat to any player who scored a hat-trick within a limited time. After obliging in that home win, he received free overcoats for himself and for the man who signed him on Athletic's books!

After a disagreement about him continuing to live in Southport, Jimmy Fay left the Latics for Bolton Wanderers.

He made his name in a Bolton shirt as a centre-half, but was laid up for most of 1913 with a hernia.

In April 1919, when he was 35, he represented the Football League against the Scottish League at Ibrox. He had another two years at Burnden before returning to Southport Central where he had played at the outbreak of World War One.

He was secretary of the PFA from 1922 to 1952 (and chairman 1922–9) having been a founder-member of the old Players' Union in 1907. Fay continued to operate his sports outfitting business and became a JP earning himself the title of 'Gentleman' James Fay. He died in his home town in March 1957.

First Division

The Latics gained promotion to the First Division in 1910 and enjoyed nine seasons in the top flight. In 1915 when the club finished second, they were robbed of the League Championship when they lost 0–2 at Liverpool. The club were then level on points with Everton—but the Toffees had one game still to play. They then drew 2–2 at home to Chelsea to take the title.

The club had a tough baptism on their return to the First Division after a 68-year absence. The tendency to present rival teams with 'soft goals' was the main contributory factory to the Latics' inconsistency in 1991–92. Their problem that season was their generosity towards opponents, especially in away games, for at home they were capable of scoring goals as well as giving them away.

Their 42 matches delivered 130 goals. Oldham score, three or more on seven occasions and conceded three or more in seven matches.

These figures merged in two games—a 6–3 home defeat by Manchester United and a 4–3 win against Notts County.

The club's record in the First Division is:

P	W	D	L	F	A
400	137	106	157	499	571

First Matches

Oldham Athletic's first game under their name was a friendly on 2 September 1899 against Berry's Reserves, a team of shoe blackers from Manchester. The game began half an hour late and Oldham began a man short, though he turned up later in a 1–0 win for Athletic. At the end of the season, Oldham needed to beat Newton Heath Clarence to win the Manchester Alliance League, but fielded only seven players and lost 2–0 to finish third.

The Latics' historic first match in the Football League was away to Stoke City on 9 September 1907 and, on the face of it, was to be one of the mis-matches of the season.

The Stoke side had spent the majority of its professional life in the First Division, whilst the Latics were unheard of only a few years previously. The Oldham team on that momentous day was—Hewitson, Hudson, Hamilton, Fay, Walders (Captain), Wilson, Ward, Dodds, Newton, Hancock and Swarbrick.

After the Potters had a goal disallowed for offside, Dodds converted a Hancock cross to put the Latics 1–0 up. That score stood until early in the second half when Watkins levelled the scores. In the final few minutes Newton headed Oldham into the lead, and in the final minute Dodds scored his second and Oldham's third goal by shooting past Box.

First Minute Goals

Bert Lister scored a goal within ten seconds of the kick-off in the 2–1 home win over Chesterfield on 13 April 1963.

The fastest ever goal in first-class soccer was scored by ex-Oldham Athletic centre-forward Jim Fryatt, then playing for Bradford Park Avenue on 25 April 1964. Just 4 seconds after the kick-off, Tranmere Rovers found themselves a goal down!

Floodlights

The floodlights at Boundary Park were switched on for the first time on Tuesday 3 October 1961 for a friendly match against Burnley. The fixture attracted a crowd of 15,520 and ended 3–3 with the Latics goals coming from Lister, Johnstone and Liddell.

The lights were paid for by public donation, and were switched on by John Clayton who had done a tremendous amount of work to get the project off the ground.

Football Association Cup

The first-ever FA Cup tie to be played in Oldham was between Oldham County and Oswaldtwistle Rovers on 31 October 1896. The first round qualifying match was won by County 7–0.

When the Latics were members of the Lancashire Combination in 1906–7, they played Liverpool, a First Division club, in the first round of the FA Cup. Oldham lost 1–0, goalkeeper Daw letting the ball roll between his legs in the last few minutes in front of a crowd of 21,000 spectators!

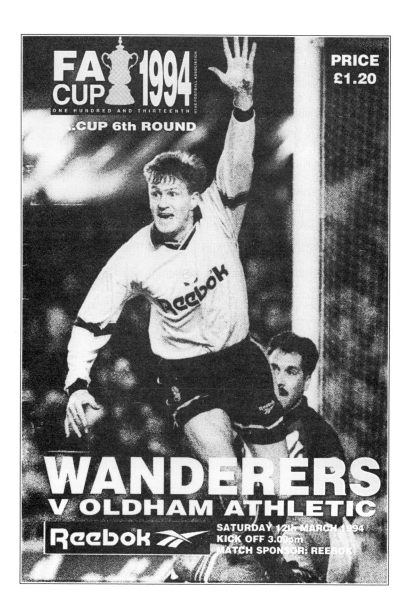

Though the Latics have never won the FA Cup, they have reached the semi-final stage on three occasions. The first of these was in 1912–13, the Latics meeting Bolton Wanderers in the third round.

After adjusting the better to the tricky conditions at a snow-covered Boundary Park, the Latics beat the Trotters 2–0 with both goals coming from Oliver Tummon. Home advantage was again put to full use in round four when Notts Forest were beaten 5–1. In the next round, Latics were held 0–0 at Boundary Park by Manchester United and it looked as if that would be the end of the road. However, four days later, the Latics made the short trip to Old Trafford and pulled off the shock result so far in the competition—a 2–1 win with goals from Gee and Toward.

The form books were upset again in the sixth round as Arthur Gee scored the only goal of the game to put the Latics in the semi-final for the first time in their history.

Drawn against Aston Villa (who had beat them 7–1 on Boxing Day) at Ewood Park (where Blackburn at also beat the Latics 7–1) it looked like a lost cause.

The game was a typical English cup-tie with the action changing from end to end. However, the game was settled in the 32nd minute when Villa's Stephenson scored the only goal of the match.

When Oldham replayed their second round FA Cup tie with Crewe Alexandra at Boundary Park in December 1949, the ground was so heavy and muddy that the Oldham players went through 24 pairs of shorts and 26 jerseys during the game!

In 1976–77, Northwich Victoria were forced to transfer their home fourth round FA Cup tie against the Latics to Maine Road, when it was discovered that they had sold more tickets than their official capacity allowed. The Latics won the game 3–1 with two goals from Vic Halom and one from Carl Valentine.

The Latics FA Cup campaign of 1989–90 started with wins over Birmingham and Brighton to set up a fascinating contest against manager Joe Royle's old club, Everton.

Held 2–2 at Boundary Park, the Latics came away from the replay at Goodison Park with a 1–1 draw, with Kevin Sheedy scoring a penalty to save the home side. In the second replay, it was Everton old boy Ian Marshall who fired the Latics into the FA Cup quarter-finals for the first time in 77 years with an extra-time penalty in a 2–1 win. The club's incredible cup exploits continued, for in round six First Division leaders Aston Villa were swept aside 3–0.

There then followed two epic encounters in the semi-final at Maine Road with Manchester United. On Sunday 8 April 1990, 44,026 witnessed the most gripping of matches in which the football was of the highest quality. From the moment that Earl Barrett broke the ice with an early goal, right through a nerve-wracking 30 minutes of extra-time this was a cup-tie to savour.

It may have been United's 18th appearance in an FA Cup semi-final and only Latics second, but the 3–3 scoreline was probably a fair result, for on the day nobody really deserved to lose. Three days later, it was Chadderton-born Mark Robins who shattered the Latics Wembley dream by snatching the winner after extra-time in a 2–1 win for the Reds.

In the 1993–94 competition, the Latics bucked the trend by being the FA Carling Premiership side that knocked out four Endsleigh Insurance League Division One teams: Derby County at home in the third round, Stoke City at the Victoria Ground after a replay and Barnsley at home in the fifth round. There then came a tough local derby away at Bolton, where a Darren Beckford goal separated the teams.

Reaching the semi-final stages again, the Latics played Manchester United. After a goal-less 90 minutes, it was Neil Pointon who broke the deadlock to give Latics the lead, only for Mark Hughes to equalise in the last minute of extra-time. In the replay at Maine Road Pointon again scored for the Latics, only for United to hit four in reply!

Football League Cup

Sad to relate, the Latics have failed to make much impact upon the Football League (later Milk, Littlewoods, Rumbelows and Coca Cola) Cup, with of course the exception of 1989–90 when the club reached the final.

Having been beaten 6–2 by Norwich City in the first season of the competition, this experience was a foretaste of things to come over the next decade. In 1962–63, Sunderland beat the Latics 7–1, whilst the following season saw Workington triumph 5–3 at Boundary Park. In

 The Latics and Notts Forest teams take to the field at Wembley in the Littlewoods Cup Final.

1969–70, Oldham visited Haig Avenue, the home of Southport, and were trounced 5–1.

But in 1989–90, Latics reached the final stage. For many Oldham fans playing League Cup ties in the New Year was a new experience, for many thought this competition came to an end in September or October!

In the 1989–90 Littlewoods Cup, the old enemy Leeds United were beaten over two legs before Latics hit the headlines by beating Scarborough 7–0 at Boundary Park, where Frankie Bunn created a new record for the competition by scoring six times. He completed his hat-trick after only 20 minutes and then scored two more before the interval as Latics turned round with a 5–0 lead. Andy Ritchie scored a sixth and then with the time going into the last minute, Frank volleyed home his record-breaker. In the next round reigning First Division champions Arsenal were beaten 3–1, and in round five another top-flight side, Southampton, were beaten after a replay.

The Latics then found themselves in the semi-finals and the focus of the national media, for alongside their Littlewood Cup success, the

 Frankie Bunn—he created a new record for the competition by scoring six times in Latics' 7–0 trouncing of Scarborough.

club were also launching a bid for the FA Cup, where they were eventually eliminated in the semi-final after two matches with Manchester United.

In the home-leg of the two-legged semi-final, the Latics massacred West Ham United 6–0 and though they were defeated 3–0 at Upton Park, it was a result that guaranteed the club a first-ever Wembley visit.

Andy Ritchie scored two of Oldham's goals in that first-leg to take his tally for the club in the competition to 13, smashing Bert Lister's total of six which had stood as the club record since 1963.

The town was virtually closed on Sunday 29 April 1990, but unfortunately one goal from Nigel Jemson broke the Latics' hearts and gave Nottingham Forest the cup. On Monday Athletic returned to town for a Civic Reception, and an estimated 60,000 turned out to watch an open-topped bus ride through the streets.

Oldham's record to date in the Football League Cup is:

P	W	D	L	F	A
85	31	16	38	138	148

 Replacing the old Broadway Stand, the Ford stand was named after the sponsors of the Sporting League, won by Latics in the 1970–71 season.

Ford Sporting League

The Ford Sporting League was based on points for good behaviour and goals scored. Sponsored by the Motor Company, it lasted for only one season—1970–71. Oldham Athletic won it easily and received £70,000 for their efforts. For good measure, the club also won promotion to Division Three and they did it in first-choice orange shirts.

The rules of the Ford Sporting League said Athletic must spend the money on ground improvements, which they did, while at the same time they had to approach the local council for financial help in running the team and the club.

Foreign Players

The Latics have fielded few foreign players, though a number of foreign-born players have been on Oldham's books (Doug Anderson—Hong Kong; Bill Andrews—Kansas City; George Hunter—Peshawar, India; Darren McDonough—Antwerp).

The first foreign player to represent the club was Ryszard Kowenicki who signed for £12,000 from Polish side Widzew Lodz in December 1979. The second, Gunnar Halle, joined Athletic for a reported £250,000 from Lillestrom in January 1991. Gunnar's international exploits with Norway have been well documented in recent years. A brief appearance by Dutchman Orfeo Keizersweerd in the second half of Athletic's game at Liverpool in April 1993 completes the list.

One player with a foreign name was John Sleeuwenhoek, the son of a Dutch parachute instructor, but he was in fact born in Wednesford!

Ryszard Kowenicki—the first foreign player at the club, he was signed from Polish side Widzew Lodz for £12,000.

Gunnar Halle—he joined Oldham from Lillestrom, Norway in January 1991 for £250,000.

Fourth Division

At the end of the 1957–58 season, the bottom 12 clubs in each of the regionalised Third Divisions would become the founder members of the new Fourth Division.

The Latics finished 15th in the Northern Secion, missing the safety mark by just one point.

In 1958–59 the club finished the season the bottom four of the Fourth Division and had to apply for re-election. However, the following season the Latics finished second from the bottom of the Division—the club really at their lowest ebb.

In 1960–61, the club had ten successive victories, but the run of wins couldn't last and they finished the campaign in a respectable 12th place. In 1961–62, the club's chances of promotion slipped away, whilst the promise of cup success beckoned.

Promotion finally came Athletic's way in 1962–63 as the club finished the season in second place behind Brentford.

After six seasons in the Third Division a disastrous 1968–69 campaign saw the club rejoin the Fourth Division.

Finishing the 1969–70 season in 19th place, the club narrowly avoided the embarrassment of applying for re-election again. Jimmy Frizzell was appointed manager and in 1970–71, the club gained promotion with 59 points and third place.

The club's record in the Fourth Division is:

P	W	D	L	F	A
320	121	70	129	499	513

Jimmy Frizzell

A prominent figure in Oldham Athletic's post-war history, Jimmy Frizzell joined the club from Morton in 1960.

Although he was originally an inside-forward, he was at home in almost any position. In seasons 1961–62 and 1964–65 he was the club's leading goalscorer, though he was later converted to wing-half and later still, to full-back.

Jimmy Frizzell became manager, first on a temporary basis and then, after distinguishing himself, on a two-year contract.

In his first full season in charge, the club won promotion from the Fourth Division and scooped £70,000 prize money from the Ford Motor Company Sporting League. Steady and continued progress saw the club finish 11th in 1971–72, fourth in 1972–73 and Third Divison champions in 1973–74, setting the Latics on a long run in Division Two.

On 15 June 1982, Athletic dropped a bombshell by dispensing with Jimmy Frizzell's services as 22 years as player and manager. Protests poured in and demonstrations were held in the town amid calls for a boardroom takeover.

At the time of his sensational sacking, Jimmy Frizzell was the second longest-serving manager in the Football League. If any proof of the Scotsman's popularity was needed, it came when 6,041 spectators attended his testimonial match, which was 2,000 more than the average league attendance at Boundary Park that season!

After a year out of work, he was appointed assistant to Manchester City's manager Billy McNeill, taking over when the former Celtic player moved to Aston Villa. In the close season of 1987, he was moved to the post of general manager, following City's relegation from the First Division.

Oldham's full league record under Jimmy Frizzell (including spell as caretaker manager) is:

P	W	D	L	F	A
542	200	162	180	727	700

Full Members Cup

The Latics only game in this competition was played in front of a crowd of 3,074 at Boundary Park on 16 September 1986 when Derby County were the visitors—the Latics going down to the only goal of the game.

Gainsborough Trinity

Gainsborough Trinity spent 16 seasons all in the Second Division between 1896 and 1912, without ever managing to finish any higher than sixth.

They met the Latics on six occasions in Oldham's first three seasons in the Football League, drawing one and losing five.

Frank Newton hit a hat-trick in Latics 4–1 win the first time the two teams met, whilst a Harry Watts goal secured a point in a 1–1 draw later in the season. In 1908–09, Latics won again by 4–1, this time away

from home and then won the return 2–0—a scoreline that stood in both the 1909–10 fixtures.

Gate Receipts

In 1910–11, Oldham's first season in Division One, the crowds against attractive opposition were at a healthy level yet the gate receipts had taken quite an alarming nose-dive.

Asked to investigate, a member of the board posted himself outside the ground for the next home game. To his amazement, he discovered that young men well past school-leaving age were passing through the boys' entrance for half price.

At the next home game, the following notice appeared:

> Boys Enter Here
> Admission 3*d*.
>
> Boys with Whiskers—
> Two Turnstiles Up
> Admission 6*d*.

As you can imagine, receipts quickly soared back to their previous level.

Gateshead

Gateshead joined the Second Divison as South Shields Adelaide in 1919. They subsequently dropped the word Adelaide from their name and in 1930–31, the club moved to Gateshead and adopted their new name.

Oldham first met the club known as South Shields on 3 November 1923, and won 1–0 with Bert Watson scoring the goal. In the ten meetings between the clubs, Latics remained undefeated at home but only won one match away from home.

Latics met Gateshead on 34 occasions with the results being fairly even. The highest scoring encounter between the two sides came in 1947–48 when Oldham won at Gateshead by 5–3. The last time the sides met was in April 1960 when Gateshead won their home match 2–0.

After 34 seasons, they failed to be re-elected in 1959–60, despite finishing third from bottom of the Fourth Division and with six points more than the bottom club, Hartlepool United.

Eric Gemmell

Eric Gemmell was a tall, stylish, strong-shooting forward. He held the Oldham front-line together splendidly and until Roger Palmer broke his record, was the club's highest aggregate goalscorer.

He made his debut for the club in the 5–1 home defeat by Rotherham United on 26 August 1947!

The first of his nine hat-tricks for the club came on 17 March 1951, when the Latics crushed Stockport County at Edgeley Park by 4–1. The following season, he scored 28 goals in 37 league appearances, including hat-tricks against Tranmere Rovers (Home 3–0) Lincoln City (Home 4–1) and Carlisle United (Away 3–3).

However, his most remarkable feat that season was his seven goals (six in succession) in the match against Chester on 19 January 1952. It was the best individual performance in the Football League since Joe Payne obtained ten in one game for Luton Town in April 1936.

Gemmell was then 30-years old, hair-line receding, but at the peak of his career. He lost count of his personal tally, as the Latics won 11–2, although Chester's Peter Greenwood, a Lancashire cricketer aware of the whip-round practice for high-scoring batsmen, told him he needed only two more for a collection!

In 1952–53 when Oldham won the Third Division (North) championship, he was restricted by injury to just 27 league appearances. Nevertheless, he scored 23 goals, including hat-tricks at Darlington (5–0) and at home to Hartlepool United (4–2) and Tranmere Rovers (5–2).

Ginger Group

At the end of the 1949–50 season in which Latics finished eleventh in the Third Division (North), a storm was raging over the so-called 'Ginger Group' of the Shareholders Association. Their published aim was to attempt changes in the constitution of the board of directors.

The group had snapped up as many shares as possible and hoped to force voting decisions through at the club's annual meeting.

However, on the night of the annual meeting of 600 shareholders, the three retiring directors, Arthur Barlow, William Bloor and Herbert Shepherd were all re-elected.

Glossop North East

Glossop North East won promotion to the First Division at the end of their first season in the League, 1898–99.

In Latics first season in the Football League the two clubs first met at Boundary Park, playing out a goal-less draw. The return match at Glossop on the final day of the season saw a similar scoreline, yet Latics finished third and Glossop 17th. The following season, both clubs won their home game by 2–1 with Frank Newton scoring both Latics goals.

The season of 1909–10 was the last time the two clubs met in the Football League. On 27 December, Glossop thrashed the Latics 6–2, but five days later on 1 January Jimmy Broad scored the only goal of the game to give Latics the two points.

The Glossop side finished bottom of the Second Division table in the last season before World War One, 1914–15 and resigned from the League shortly before the resumption of matches in 1919.

Goalkeepers

Oldham Athletic Football Club has almost always been extremely well served by its goalkeepers, and most of them have been highly popular with the supporters.

Bob Hewitson was Latics' first goalkeeper in the Football League. In 1907–08 he was suspended by the FA following an ill-tempered match against Fulham when he was alleged to have thrown a lump of turf at the referee.

In Latics' last season of non-league football, the club played Kidderminster in an FA Cup tie. The referee awarded a penalty against Oldham. Placing the ball on the spot, he turned round to find there was no goalkeeper. Hewitson was behind the goal among the fans, laying the odds that they would not score—and they didn't!

Howard Matthews was the son of a well-known amateur goalkeeper. A fine player, who many senior supporters rate above the club's full international goalkeepers, he was a life-long teetotaller and non-smoker and made 344 league appearances for the Latics.

Albert Gray is Latics' most capped player, with 9 Welsh international appearances while at Boundary Park. A goalkeeper whose tremendous

Andy Goram—now with Rangers, he became Latics' first World Cup player when called into Scotland's squad for the 1986 Finals in Mexico.

reach, agility and courage were the principal features of his play, there have been none better.

Signed from Fleetwood, after Blackpool had given him a free-transfer, Jack Hacking proved wonderfully consistent throughout his eight seasons at Boundary Park. He made 223 league appearances for the Latics before moving to Manchester United, where he produced a succession of inspired performances to ensure the Reds' Second Division status.

Whilst George Bradshaw was one of the club's oldest debutants at 37 years 162 days, it seems likely that Eddie Hopkinson, who was to make his name with Bolton Wanderers and England, was the youngest at 16 years 75 days. In an 18-year career at Burnden Park, he set up a new appearance record with 519 League and 59 FA Cup appearances. Though he only played in three games for Oldham, they were remarkable for the number of goals scored—(Latics first) 1–3, 11–2 and 0–5.

Fred and Chris Ogden are the only father and son to keep goal for Oldham whilst Andy Goram was a worthy successor to Latics' international goalkeepers of yesteryear. Winning his first cap against East Germany in 1986, he became only the third Athletic player to be capped by Scotland.

Goalscoring

For the club:

The Latics' highest goalscoring tally was achieved in 1962–63 when the team which had won promotion from Division Four hit 95 goals in 46 matches, including eleven against Southport on Boxing Day.

By the individual:

The following players have scored 50 or more League goals for the club.

Roger Palmer	1980–1994	141
Eric Gemmell	1947–1954	109
David Shaw	1969–1978	91
Andy Ritchie	1987–1994	70

Bert Watson	1921–1929	64
Ray Haddington	1947–1950	63
Don Travis	1951–1957	62
Matthew Gray	1928–1945	58
Jimmy Frizzell	1960–1969	57
Tommy Davis	1935–1938	51
Albert Pynegar	1925–1929	51
Rodger Wylde	1980–1983	51

All dates refer to calendar years of debuts and last appearances.
Correct to August 1994.

 Roger Palmer breaks the club's goalscoring record when he hit the target against Ipswich town on 4 April 1989.

Ted Goodier

Ted Goodier took charge at Boundary Park immediately following the Whitsuntide holidays in 1956.

It was at Boundary Park where he obtained his first real opportunity as a player in the 1920s. Making his debut at Fulham on 23 January

1926, he went on to give consistent and meritorious service until late in 1931 when he left because of a disagreement over a benefit.

His previous management experience included a lengthy spell at Rochdale, where helped to put the club on its feet and at Wigan Athletic, where he saw the non-league club carry all before them and earn national recognition when holding Newcastle United to a 2–2 draw at St James' Park on the Third Round of the FA Cup in 1953–54.

In his first season at Boundary Park he used 31 players, of which no fewer than 19 were new signings. The side finished a disappointing 19th winning only two of their last 28 matches.

The side began the 1957–58 season badly and though they recovered to remain undefeated for a run of 12 games, they won only once during the first three months of 1958 and eventually became founder-members of the Fourth Division.

Having failed to arrest the Latics' slide into soccer's basement, he left the club for the last time in the close season.

Oldham's full league record under Ted Goodier was:

P	W	D	L	F	A
92	26	32	34	138	158

Guest Players

The 'guest' system was used by all clubs during the two Wars. Although at times it was abused almost beyond belief (in that some sides that opposed Oldham had ten or eleven guests!) it normally worked sensibly and effectively to the benefit of the players, clubs and supporters alike.

In the First World War, some Latics players drifted to Lancashire clubs—Jimmy Broad to Blackburn and Hugh Lester to Liverpool. Stephen Buxton who played for Athletic until his transfer to Darlington in 1913 returned to 'guest' for the club in the last wartime season, when he was serving in the RAMC.

In the Second World War, two 'guest' players stand out. Arthur Buckley's early days at Boundary Park were a struggle. In fact, he waited over two years for his League debut, but after winning a first-team spot, he was transferred to Leeds United. He remained first-choice at Elland Road until the outbreak of World War Two, during which he 'guested' for the Latics.

Tommy Butler was transferred to Middlesbrough in the latter part of the 1938–39 season, but was soon back at Boundary Park 'guesting' for Latics. This led to him rejoining the club for the first post-war season.

George Hardwick

England's captain in the immediate post-war years, George Hardwick was a born leader who skippered for every team for which he played. He appeared in three wartime Cup Finals for Chelsea at Wembley and Stamford Bridge and became, in November 1950, Latics' youngest-ever manager.

The player-boss attracted 21,742 spectators to Boundary Park for his debut, marking a new and exciting era for the club.

Hardwick lifted the Oldham side from 21st to a position of mid-table by the end of his first season. In 1951–52, new signing Peter McKennan (from Middlesbrough) and Jack Warner (from Manchester United) brought a great improvement in the Oldham side and they finished fourth, 12 points adrift of Lincoln City who won the championship.

He continued to exert great influence on the Oldham side and in 1952–53, the club won the Third Division (North) Championship. Though Eric Gemmell hit three hat-tricks, it was an improved defensive performance which led to the team clinching the title.

The usual lack of finance precluded any significant strengthening of the side and by the middle of the season, relegation looked certain, as indeed it was.

Any hopes of a speedy return were dashed by a poor start to the 1954–55 campaign, when the only bright note was the 32 goals scored by centre-forward Don Travis.

Hardwick's final season in charge saw the Latics finish 20th. It was a disappointing ending, for if funds had been found to strengthen the

 George Hardwick—England's captain in the immediate post-war years, he became Oldham's youngest-ever manager.

side in 1953–54 to consolidate the promotion to Division Two, things could well have turned out differently.

Oldham's full league record under George Hardwick was:

P	W	D	L	F	A
256	95	66	95	403	389

Hat-tricks

The club's first hat-trick in the Football League came from Frank Newton in the 4–1 win over Gainsborough Trinity on 14 December 1907.

In 1909–10, Jimmy Fay was moved out of defence to bolster the attack. In 21 matches he banged in 26 goals, including a hat-trick against Barnsley which earned him a new overcoat from a local tailor!

Maurice Wellock made a sensational debut for Athletic at Grimsby on 12 February 1927 when he scored four goals in a 5–2 win. Yet, remarkably he remained at Boundary Park for only three months, being one of six centre-forwards tried that season.

In 1936–37, Tommy Davis scored four hat-tricks in the League and another against Barrow in the Third Division (North) Cup. Jack 'Legs' Diamond scored a first-half hat-trick in Oldham's pre-season public trial of 1938. Switching sides at half-time after Tommy Davis was injured, Diamond netted another three, yet still finished on the losing side!

Another Oldham player to mark his debut for the club with a hat-trick was Dave Pearson, who hit three goals in the 4–3 defeat of Halifax Town on 21 August 1956.

Making his debut for Athletic's Reserve side on 19 August 1961, Len Dickinson scored five goals which included a seven-minute hat-trick. One of Latics' most prolific goalscoring centre-forwards of all time, Bert Lister, hit six goals in the 11–0 Boxing Day win of 1962 over Southport. He also suffered the misfortune of having a hat-trick 'cancelled' in Oldham's inaugural floodlit match at Boundary Park on 11 October 1961. The opponents, Accrington Stanley, failed to last out

 Graeme Sharp—the last Oldham player to score a hat-trick when he scored four of Latics' goals in the 5–1 win over Luton town on 11 April 1992.

the season and on their resignation all matches played by the Peel Park outfit were expunged from the records.

Tony Foster was the star of the Latics' summer tour of Rhodesia and Malawi in 1967 with 11 goals, including six in one match.

Frankie Bunn achieved what no other player had been able to do during the 30-year history of the Football League Cup when he scored six goals in Latics' 7–0 win over Scarborough on 25 October 1989.

However, it is Eric Gemmell who holds the individual goalscoring record, notching seven goals (six in succession) in the match against Chester on 19 January 1952 as Latics won 11–2.

There have been two occasions when two Oldham players have scored hat-tricks in the same match. The first came in 1925–26 when Albert Pynegar (4) and Frank Hargreaves (3) helped Latics to an 8–3 home win over Notts Forest. The second in 1934–35 saw Matthew Gray and Bill Walsh help themselves to three goals apiece as Bury went down 7–2.

The last Oldham player to score a hat-trick in the Football League was Graeme Sharp, who scored four of Latics' goals in a 5–1 home win over Luton Town on 11 April 1992.

Highest Scoring Game

On Christmas Day 1935, Oldham Athletic beat the Third Division (North) table-toppers Tranmere Rovers by 4–1. However, when the two teams met the following day at Prenton Park, Oldham again scored four times past the Tranmere defence, but unfortunately for the Latics, the home team found the net thirteen times!

Tranmere's Bunny Bell scored nine goals and missed a penalty! A director of the Wirral club suggested the run of the game would have been best underlined by a 17–0 scoreline, for in addition to Bell's penalty miss, a number of 'open goals' went begging, while there was some excellent goalkeeping at both ends.

Home Matches

Not including the pre-Football League matches, Latics best home wins were the 11–0 rout of Southport in a Division Four match on Boxing Day 1962, and the 11–2 victory over Chester in a Divison Three (North) game on 19 January 1952.

On 28 November 1925, Latics beat Lytham 10–1 in the Third Round of the FA Cup. In the club's first season in the Football League, Division Two, they beat Darwen 8–1, but that too was in the FA Cup. The Latics also hit eight goals in an 8–3 victory over Nottingham Forest in the final fixture of the 1925–26 campaign.

More recently, Oldham beat Torquay United 7–1 in the Football League Cup, one of eight occasions that the Latics have scored seven goals in a home fixture. They kept a clean sheet in two of those victories—Hull City 1933–34; and Scarborough 1989–90 in the League Cup.

Latics worst home defeat was the 6–0 thrashing handed out to them by Aston Villa on 27 November 1971.

Home Seasons

Oldham Athletic have gone through a complete League season with an undefeated home record on just one occasion, and that was in the club's first season in the Football League, 1907–08.

Their record that season was:

P	W	D	L	F	A
19	15	4	0	53	14

There have been eight seasons when the Latics have lost just one home league games—1908–09; 1912–13; 1923–24; 1936–37; 1937–38; 1962–63; 1989–90 and 1990–91.

Oldham's highest number of home wins in a league season is 19. The club achieved this number of victories in 1951–52 from a 23 match programme.

Hudson Fold

During the 1899–1900 season, the club were in dispute with the Landlord at the Athletic Ground in Sheepfoot Lane, which resulted in them transferring to a Ground at Hudson Fold. To all intents and purposes, this was the same venue as the clubs former ground at Pine Mill.

Though the move proved to be costly, the team performed well and finished the season in third place in the Manchester Alliance. The next season, the club were elevated into the Manchester League.

Determined to succeed, the club developed the Hudson Fold Ground to a good standard for a Club at their level. In 1905, the enclosure was enlarged and embankments were formed. In addition, a small members stand and two dressing rooms had also been built.

In 1906, the Club became a Limited Company and in 1906–7 they moved back to the Athletic Stadium, a venue which eventually became known as Boundary Park.

The former Hudson Fold Ground, long since disappeared, was local adjacent to the current Westhulme Hospital, approximately where Westhulme Avenue now runs.

Gordon Hurst

Gordon Hurst, the one-time Charlton Athletic winger, actually started his career as a wartime amateur with the Latics, following two seasons with Ferranti's in the Manchester Amateur League.

Embarking on a distinguished career at The Valley in May 1946, he appeared in 378 First Division games and over 30 FA Cup ties including an appearance in Charlton's 1–0 success over Burnley in the Cup Final of 1947.

After a spell as player-manager at Tunbridge Wells and three seasons as coach of Llandudno, he returned to Oldham to work for the local council in 1963. The following year, he took charge, on a part-time basis of Oldham's reserve side.

A surprise choice for the Latics hot-seat in May 1965, he began under the handicap of having lost players of the calibre of Alan Williams and Peter McCall. The side struggled and only recorded three wins in 22 League matches before Jimmy McIlroy took over. Hurst continued as assistant before joining Rochdale as trainer coach in July 1967.

Oldham's full league record under Gordon Hurst is:

P	W	D	L	F	A
22	3	7	12	28	54

International Players

Latics' most capped player (ie: caps gained while players were registered with the club) is Bert Gray with 9 caps. The following is a complete list of players who have gained full international honours while at Boundary Park.

England	caps	Republic of Ireland	caps
J. Hacking	3	T. L. Davis	2
H. Moffatt	1	M. Milligan	1
G. Woodger	1		
		Wales	
Northern Ireland		D. W. Davies	2
R. V. Blair	5	A. Gray	9
L. Cumming	1	E. Jones	4
T. L. Davis	1		
W. C. Johnston	1	*Norway*	
		G. Halle	
Scotland			
J. Donnachie	3	Latics' first player to be	
A. L. Goram	4	capped was George 'Lady'	
D. Wilson	1	Woodger who played for	
		England *v.* Ireland at Derby	
		on 11 February 1911	

Bobby Johnstone

Bobby Johnston, arch-schemer and creator of so many wonderful moments, became a legend during his spell at Boundary Park.

Born in Selkirk, Bobby began his career with Hibernian in the Scottish League and moved south of the border for a £20,000 fee to join Manchester City in March 1955. He made 120 appearances for City as well as scoring in two successive FA Cup Finals—he scored the winning goal in 1956—before returning to Hibernian in 1959.

He came to Boundary Park in October 1960 for a bargain fee of £4,000 and was an instant hit because of his flair for creating goals and instinctive ability to control any game from the centre circle. He had the brilliant knack of creating goals with a single defence-splitting pass and soon had the Oldham crowd baying in appreciation.

The highest Boundary Park attendance for six and a half years (17,116) saw him score in his debut game against Exeter City in a 5–2 win. In all, he made 17 appearances for Scotland—surprisingly few

Bobby Johnstone—a great schemer and ball-artist, he soon had the Boundary Park crowd baying in appreciation.

when considering his ability—and was admired over the length and breadth of Britain.

The architect of many wonderful wins and the creator of countless magical moments in football—Bobby Johnstone can be compared favourably with the likes of Mannion and Docherty as a schemer and ball-artist.

The kind of player that, on today's transfer market, would probably fetch millions of pounds.

Junior Latics

Membership of the Junior Latics in open to boys and girls aged 7–16 years. On enrolling, the fans received a package of Latics Souvenirs, in addition to all the other benefits available to Junior Latic Members. These include:

Regular meetings at the Queen Elizabeth Hall where Junior Latics get the opportunity to meet the players and be drawn out as Match Mascot.

A Bumper Christmas Party with entertainment and a buffet supper provided.

A Birthday Card signed by Joe Royle sent to all Junior Latics members.

An indoor soccer tournament which runs for five weeks during the months of March and April.

Selected away trips where Junior Latics can play football against other Premier League club's Junior Supporters.

"Keep the Ball Rolling"

Produced in 1933, a brochure called "Keep the Ball Rolling" drew attention to the Latics' financial plight by its homilies: 'We are pulling are you?' 'We need money—let's get acquainted', 'Hats off to the past! Coats off to the future' and 'Our treasurer awaits you, with open arms'.

Lancashire Combination

The club's first season in the Lancashire Combination was 1904–05. After finishing third in the 'B' Division, they were promoted. Their biggest victory that season was 11–0 *v.* Newton-le-Willows with Shoreman netting six goals and Plumpton five.

In 1905–06, the club finished thirteenth in the 'A' Division, but in 1906–07, pipped both Liverpool Reserves and Everton Reserves to win the Combination Championship.

Largest Crowd

It was on 25 January 1930 that Boundary Park housed its largest crowd. The occasion was the FA Cup Fourth Round match against Sheffield Wednesday. The crowd of 46,471 witnessed the most exciting of cup-ties. Though the Latics exerted energetic pressure for the first five minutes, it was Wednesday who took the lead through Hooper. Stewart Littlewood equalised after 22 minutes and did so again just before half-time after Allen had given the visitors the lead.

In the 53rd minute, Les Adlam's deflected shot gave Oldham the lead and hope of victory. However, it wasn't to be as Jimmy Seed headed an equaliser following Ellis Rimmer's deep cross and then with virtually the last kick of the game, Allen grabbed his second and Wednesday's fourth to clinch the game for the Owls.

Late Finishes

Oldham's latest finish to a Football League season was 26 May 1947 when the club visited Millmoor the home of Rotherham United and lost 0–8!

During the war many curious things occured, and in 1939–40, Latics last match in the North West Division of the War Regional League saw them beat Blackpool 4–2 at Boundary Park on 8 June 1940, with Ron Ferrier scoring two of the goals.

Leading Goalscorers

Tommy Davis—holder of the club's individual scoring record with 35 League and Cup goals in 1936–37.

The best indivdual scoring record for one season with Oldham Athletic was Tommy Davis's 35 League and Cup goals in 1936–37.

In later years, Don Travis came closest to the record with 34 goals in 1954–55, whilst Bert Lister hit 33 in 1962–63.

Leeds City

Founder members of the Second Division in 1892, Leeds City were never promoted during their Football League career.

The two clubs met on six occasions in Latics' first three seasons in the Football League. After completing the 'double' over their Yorkshire opponents in 1907–08, Frank Newton hit a hat-trick in a 6–0 home win the following season before Latics went down 3–0 in the return match. In 1909–10, the Latics completed the 'double' again, including a 5–3 win at Leeds.

The club were expelled from the League in 1919 after making illegal payments during wartime matches.

J. W. Lees Brewery

In the early part of the twentieth century, J. W. Lees Brewery from nearby Middleton Junction, began an involvement with the club.

They leased out the present site of the ground at Sheepfoot Lane to the club and that was the beginning of an association which has continued to this day when J. W. Lees are now the major shareholders.

In the early 1980s, many Football League clubs were feeling the pinch as a countrywide recession saw 17% unemployment figures in Oldham. Striving to survive and finding it difficult to keep afloat, the club were assisted by J. W. Lees Brewery.

A package deal involving the Brewery buying the Boundary Club and Sports Hall Complex and discharging the Club's bank overdraft, loans and other debts, was agreed. The deal was worth over half-a-million for which the Brewery had a five-year sponsorship package for ground, programme and shirt advertising and Latics had time to reorganise and settle the debt.

Lowest

The lowest number of goals scored by Oldham Athletic in a single Football League season is 35 in seasons 1922–23 (when the club were relegated from Division One) and 1924–25.

The lowest points record in the Football League occured in 1953–54, when Latics gained just 25 points from 42 matches to finish bottom of the Second Division.

Managers

This is the complete list of Latics' full-time managers with the inclusive dates in which they held office. Biographies of those who have made major contributions to the club are included in alphabetical order in this A-Z.

David Ashworth	1906–14	George Hardwick	1950–6
Herbert Bamlett	1914–21	Ted Goodier	1956–8
Charlie Roberts	1921–2	Norman Dodgin	1958–60
David Ashworth	1923–4	Jack Rowley	1960–3
Bob Mellor	1924–7	Les McDowall	1963–5
Andy Wilson	1927–2	Gordon Hurst	1965–6
Jimmy McMullan	1933–4	Jimmy McIlroy	1966–8
Bob Mellor	1934–45	Jack Rowley	1968–9
Frank Womack	1945–7	Jimmy Frizzell	1970–82
Billy Wootton	1947–50	Joe Royle	1982–

Manchester Alliance League

Oldham Athletic came into the world at the Black Cow Inn on Burnley Lane, Chadderton on 4 July 1899. Formerly known as Pine Villa, the club took over Oldham County's old ground.

Though the club had teething problems, the first president George Elliot and his committee dug deep into their pockets to keep the club alive. Having applied to the Manchester Alliance League, they collected a good team of amateurs and set off with a vengeance.

Their first match in the Manchester Alliance League was against Nook Rovers, which the club won 4–2, although a week earlier, the 'Latics' as they were now known had beaten Berry's Reserves in a friendly 1–0.

Their only season in the Manchester Alliance League saw them finish third in the table and reach the final of the Manchester Alliance Cup, where they went down 3–1 to Failsworth Springfield. However, on the final day of the season, the club needed to beat Newton Heath Clarence to win the Manchester Alliance League. They turned up with only seven men and lost 2–0!

Manchester City

The rivalry between Oldham Athletic and Manchester City stretches right back to the Latics early days in the Football League.

The first visit of Manchester City to Boundary Park in a league game was on 13 November 1909. A beautiful sunny day for the 25,000 crowd saw a Cook penalty defeat City, who were at the time second in the table. In fact, goals by Fay and Toward saw Latics win 2–0 at Maine Road later in the season, to complete the 'double'.

Before Manchester City visited Boundary Park on Good Friday 1984, you had to go back 56 years to find the last occasion that the Citizens visited Oldham for a league game.

At the end of that 1927–28 season, City returned to the First Division as Second Division champions, managing to score 100 goals and winning the league with 59 points, two clear of Leeds United. Athletic finished in 7th position, winning 3–2 at Boundary Park, but losing 3–1 at Maine Road.

The first fixture of the 1983–84 season saw City win 2–0 at home, but we can only imagine what the result would have been if Roger Palmer's shot at the start of the second half had counted. With the game goal-less at this point, Roger hammered in a shot from the edge of the City penalty area, but saw the ball hit the underside of the bar and bounce down on the line before being cleared.

However, Roger did get his revenge in the match at Maine Road in the 1988–89 season, hitting a hat-trick as Latics won 4–1.

There have been many players who have played for both clubs, including: Earl Barrett, Kenny Clements, Willie Donachie, Harry Dowd, Paul and Ron Futcher, Eric Gemmell, Bert Gray, Ray

Haddington, Tony Henry, Bobby Johnstone, Ged Keegan and of course Roger Palmer.

There have also been connections on the managerial side with Latics boss Joe Royle having made 99 league appearances for City and former boss Jimmy Frizzell joining the club as assistant manager to Billy McNeill.

Manchester League

Following their performance in the Manchester Alliance League, the Latics were now ready for much bigger games and in 1900–01 joined the semi-professional Manchester League.

Their first game at home to Middleton drew a sizeable crowd—Latics winning 1–0. However, halfway through the season came a setback. Trouble arose with the grounds landlord over the terms of lease and the rent and, because no compromise could be reached, the only answer was for Latics to find another ground on which to play their matches.

Hudson Fold was chosen and though the move proved a costly one, as a stand had to be erected for members, plenty willing helpers kept the club alive.

Latics stayed in the Manchester League for four seasons. In each of those seasons, their league placing showed an improvement—twelfth, sixth, fourth and third and in 1903, they won the Manchester Junior Cup, defeating Berry's 1–0 in the Final.

Manchester United

Latics' meetings with Manchester United have always been something special, the highlight of the season's calendar.

The two clubs met for the first time on 19 November 1910, when the Reds won 3–1 at Boundary Park. Seven of the next eight encounters were drawn, including the FA Cup fifth round match at Boundary

 Earl Barratt breaks the ice with an early goal in the F.A. Cup semi-final match with Manchester United on 8 April 1990.

Park on 22 February 1913. Four days later, Athletic made the short trip to Old Trafford and put up a tremendous, battling display to pull off the shock result so far in the competition . . . a 2–1 win with goals from Gee and Toward.

The club's first wartime match was played on 4 September 1915 against Manchester United at Boundary Park. Oldham won 3–2 in front of 4,420 with takings of £99 at a 'Tanner' a time.

The club made the headlines on 6 October 1923 in the Division Two fixture at Boundary Park. Sam Wynne scored with a penalty and a free-kick for Oldham and also scored two own-goals for Manchester United. Billy Howson scored the Latics other goal, as they ran out winners 3–2. In season 1931–32, United completed the 'double' over Latics for the first time, winning both matches 5–1!

On 28 December 1974, top-of-the-table Manchester United had only lost three of their 24 Second Division games when they visited Boundary Park. Athletic on the other hand were in the relegation zone,

but this famous 1–0 victory gave them the fillip they needed to inch their way towards safety.

The goal came from the penalty spot, but as Maurice Whittle placed the ball, the wind blew it away. The players and the crowd replayed the tense, silent scene, but next Whittle shot hard and true past an immobile Stepney.

In 1989–90, Latics and United served up two epic encounters in the semi-finals of the FA Cup. Goals from Barrett, Marshall and Palmer helped Oldham draw 3–3 in the first gripping Maine Road encounter. The Latics's dreams of reaching Wembley were shattered by Mark Robins after 110 minutes of tension and drama. Brian McClair had given United the lead, but with only 10 minutes left Andy Ritchie slotted home a first-time left-foot shot to take the game into extra-time. There are not many, if any, teams that would continue to play with five forwards and go all out for a winner as Latics did in the second period of extra-time. Most clubs would have settled for another replay, but Athletic have this lovely, refreshing approach. Unfortunately, they are liable to pay for it at times by being caught out at the back and so it proved when Robins hit the winner.

In 1992–93 when United lifted the first-ever Premier League title, the Latics again pulled off the impossible, clinching a 1–0 victory over the Reds to add to their growing confidence and throw a spanner albeit temporarily into the Championship race.

Last season of course, Latics and United met in the FA Cup semi-final at Wembley. The match itself was a dull affair and only came to life after a goal-less 90 minutes. Neil Pointon gave Oldham the lead, only for Mark Hughes to equalise with time running out. Unfortunately for the Latics, the Red Devils produced some stunning football in the Maine Road replay and won 4–1 with Neil Pointon once again scoring Oldham's goal.

There have been many players who have played for both clubs including: Martin Buchan, Paul Edwards, Ian Greaves, Jack Hacking, Denis Irwin, Andy Ritchie, Albert Quixall, Charlie Roberts and Jeff Wealands.

F.A. CUP SEMI-FINAL

OLDHAM ATHLETIC

VERSUS

MANCHESTER UNITED

Sunday, 8th April, 1990
Kick-off: 3.30 p.m.
at Maine Road, Manchester.

OFFICIAL MATCHDAY MAGAZINE
£1.00

Marketing Campaign

After pipping both Everton and Liverpool Reserves for the Lancashire Combination championship, the Latics' targeted a marketing campaign at Football League clubs.

Probably football's best example of futurism was the idea of car and window-stickers in 1907—'Oldham wants League Football'.

In addition, the club produced a detailed document for canvassing other clubs. It stated that Oldham's Municipal population was 150,000, and that within ten miles the population was 'over two-and-a-half-million'. Oldham was easily accessible to Second Division clubs; there was a 20-minute train service from Manchester and a good electric-car system.

Soccer had ousted rugby as the most popular sport. Furthermore Lancashire Combination attendances were good—'we have been able to obtain 8,000 spectators regularly'—and officials of the club claimed that the ground could hold 50,000 people.

The plan did not work. Burton United were replaced by Fulham and the Latics were left in the cold . . . until Burslem Port Vale resigned at the last minute and Oldham were invited in!

Les McDowall

Les McDowall's football career began when he was recruited by Sunderland on Christmas Eve 1932 from Glentyan Thistle, a team of unemployed men, following the loss of his job in the shipyard industry during the depression.

In March 1938, he joined Manchester City, but the war intervened and he resumed his occupation as a draughtsman in a local aircraft factory. When football restarted in 1946–47, he marshalled a fine City defence from centre-half, the team winning the Second Division championship.

He left Maine Road in June 1949 to become Wrexham's manager, but within twelve months had returned to Manchester City. Manager for the next 13 seasons, he won promotion from the Second Division in his first season in charge and later took the side to two successive FA Cup Finals, winning the trophy in 1956.

Following City's relegation from the First Division in 1963, he left and within a month had joined Oldham to take charge of a newly-promoted Latics side.

Though they led the Third Division for a spell, they eventually finished with 48 points and in ninth place. In 1964–65, only two wins were recorded in the first 17 matches, and though seven wins and a draw in nine league matches before Christmas saw them turn the tide, another slump saw them on the edge of the relegation zone by Easter.

Having failed to win a solitary away victory in 1965, the Latics parted company with Les McDowall.

Oldham's full league record under Les McDowall is:

P	W	D	L	F	A
86	32	16	38	126	142

Jimmy McIlroy

Jimmy McIlroy took charge of an Oldham side at the bottom of Division Three with only 13 points from 22 matches, after being recruited on a five-year contract by chairman Ken Bates. Guiding the team away from relegation in the 1965–66 season, he dismantled Gordon Hurst's side and rebuilt around new signings Asprey, Blore, Large, Stevens and Towers.

In 1966–67 further signings were made, including Bebbington, Best, Collins and Knighton. Despite the Latics leading the table for a spell in September, the side failed to keep up the push for promotion and finished tenth. It was a season in which McIlroy blooded several young players, amongst whom Ronnie Blair, Les Chapman and Ian Wood showed great promise for the future. The disappointment of McIlroy's first full season in charge was tempered somewhat by Latics winning the Lancashire Senior Cup, the side being the first for 60 years to bring the famous old trophy back to Boundary Park.

The following season saw the Latics finish 16th in what was an up and down campaign. Only one win in the opening 12 league matches was followed by seven consecutive wins!

The 1968–69 season had barely kicked-off when Jimmy McIlroy resigned his post as Oldham's boss to take up a new future with First Division Stoke City.

As a player, McIlroy gained 55 Northern Ireland caps and in a career at Turf Moor that spanned 13 years, he scored 114 goals in 437 games.

Oldham's full league record under Jimmy McIlroy was:

P	W	D	L	F	A
120	46	24	50	168	166

Jimmy McMullan

In charge for only one season, Jimmy McMullan took the Latics to a commendable ninth place in the Second Division. This was despite the handicap of having to transfer Jack Hacking, Cliff Chadwick and John Pears during the course of the season.

The highlight of that 1933–34 season was the two fourth round FA Cup ties against Sheffield Wednesday which attracted large crowds at both venues. The side also enjoyed a good run in the Lancashire Senior Cup, beating New Brighton 4–0, Liverpool 4–0 and Blackburn Rovers 3–1 before losing 4–2 to Bolton Wanderers in the Final at Maine Road.

Jimmy McMullan captained the immortal Wembley Wizards and with 16 full caps, four Victory International appearances and four Scottish League caps, also won a Second Division championship medal in 1928 with Manchester City after his move from Partick Thistle.

He left Oldham in May 1934 to become Aston Villa's first-ever manager, before moving to Notts County in a similar capacity in November 1936. Just over twelve months later, he moved to Sheffield Wednesday as secretary-manager.

Oldham's full league record under Jimmy McMullan was:

P	W	D	L	F	A
42	17	10	15	72	60

Bob Mellor

Bob Mellor's connection with Oldham Athletic began in 1906 when he was employed by Egbert Thompson, a local accountant, who was in charge of Latics' flotation as a limited company. It was during the 1909–10 season that the Oldham board decided to run affairs from the club's offices at Boundary Park, leading to Mellor's appointment as full-time secretary on New Year's Day 1910.

At the time of his appointment Latics were in mid-table in the Second Division, but then proceeded not to lose another match until Good Friday and won promotion to Division One!

In 43 years as Athletic's secretary, Bob Mellor was called upon to fill the dual role of secretary-manager on the three occasions below (July 1924—July 1927; July 1932—May 1933; and May 1934—February 1945).

He was always generous in his praise of Jimmy Hansen, the club's long-serving trainer, acknowledging that it was he that did as much as anyone to bring the players up to scratch, irrespective of who the club's manager was at the time.

In 1936 Mellor was awarded the Football League's Long Service Medal, the presentation being made by Charles E. Sutcliffe, a League Management Committee member who had acted as solicitor for the Latics when the company was floated in 1906.

Bob Mellor who was born at 'Waste Dealer's Arms', Botton o'th Moor, on 16 December 1877, died aged 89 in May 1967.

Oldham's full league record under Bob Mellor was:

P	W	D	L	F	A
378	154	77	147	612	615

Most Goals in a Season

Oldham Athletic scored 95 goals in 46 Division Four matches during 1962–63. They scored in every home game and only failed to score in

four away fixtures. Sixty five goals were scored at home, equalling the record that was established in the 1951–52 season.

The club's biggest win in 1962–63 was the 11–0 Boxing Day victory over Southport, whilst Hartlepool United (6–1) and Rochdale (5–1) also felt the force of Latics strike-power.

The top scorer in 1962–63 was the tenacious Bert Lister with 32 goals, whilst Colin Whitaker had 17 and John Colquhoun 14. Oldham finished the season as runners-up to Brentford and gained promotion to the Third Division.

Most Matches

The most first-class matches played by the Latics in a single season is 64 in 1989–90. This figure includes nine FA Cup and nine Football League Cup fixtures, along with the 44 Divison Two matches.

In the space of four weeks in both April 1949 and April 1955, the Latics played 10 matches.

1949			
April 2	York City	H	4–0
4	Rotherham United	A	1–2
9	Stockport County	A	2–1
12	Gateshead	H	0–0
15	Halifax Town	H	2–2
16	Carlisle United	H	1–0
18	Halifax Town	A	1–3
23	Gateshead	A	2–2
26	Hull City	H	1–1
30	Hartlepool United	H	5–1

1955			
April 2	Crewe Alexandra	A	1–4
8	Scunthorpe United	H	1–1
9	Carlisle United	H	2–1
11	Scunthorpe United	A	1–6
16	Chester	A	0–0
18	Bradford	H	5–0
20	Rochdale	A	1–2
23	Grimsby Town	H	4–0
26	Carlisle United	A	2–5
30	Bradford	A	2–0

Jimmy Naylor

One of Athletic's best-ever locally produced players, Jimmy Naylor, was associated with the club for over eight years before leaving to find First Division fame, but returned at the close of his League career and was instrumental in guiding the Latics clear of the relegation zone in 1932–33.

Jimmy Naylor always played left-half unless he was required to replace an injured colleague and during his time at Boundary Park was never dropped. In fact, in that time he missed only five games—all through injury and at one period had an ever-present record of 168 matches in four years.

He made 238 League appearances for the Latics from 1922 to the 1928–29 season when Huddersfield Town paid a then record fee received by Athletic of £3,750 for his stylish services. Naylor didn't like leaving Boundary Park and it took him almost two weeks of soul searching before agreeing to the move. It was while he was at Leeds Road that he received his international trial cap on 4 February 1928, and had the honour of shaking hands with King George V at the famous 'Zepplin' Cup Final of 1930 when Huddersfield lost to

 'Gentleman' Jimmy Naylor'—one of Latics' best-ever locally produced players.

Arsenal 0–2. In July 1930 he was transferred again, this time to north-east giants Newcastle United. He became a firm favourite on Tyneside and gave two years stirling service, the climax of which was a second Wembley appearance, but this time only as a reserve as Newcastle beat Arsenal 2–1.

In October 1932 he signed for Manchester City, but unable to command a regular first team place he was loaned back to Athletic for eight appearances during the 1932–33 season and played a major part in the successful fight against relegation that year. When City eventually freed him, he ended his playing career with stints at non-league Macclesfield, Wigan and Nelson before finally hanging up his boots in 1937.

One of the last of a rare breed of sportsmen who graced Athletic's colours during their halcyon days in the First Division, 'Gentleman' Jimmy Naylor never knowingly fouled an opponent. He died on 31 August 1983 at the age of 82.

Nelson

Founder members of the Third Division (North) in 1921–22, Nelson were champions the following season, but were relegated after just one season in Division Two.

It was during that 1923–24 Division Two campaign that the two clubs met for the only time in the Football League. Nelson won their home game 2–1, whilst a Bert Watson goal gave Latics the points in the return fixture seven days later.

Nelson spent the remainder of their League career in the Third Division (North) before losing their battle against re-election in 1930–31.

Neutral Grounds

The Latics have had to replay on a neutral ground a number of times:

Date	Opponents	Venue	FA Cup stage	Score
19 January 1950	Crewe Alexandra	Maine Road	Round 2	3–0
14 January 1974	Cambridge United	Notts Forest	Round 3	2–1
11 April 1990	Manchester United	Maine Road	Semi-Final	1–2

The club's semi-finals were of course played on neutral grounds:

Date	Opponents	Venue	Score
29 March 1913	Aston Villa	Ewood Park	0–1
8 April 1990	Manchester United	Maine Road	3–3

In 1976–77, Northwich Victoria were forced to transfer their home game in the fourth round of the FA Cup against the Latics to Maine Road, when it was discovered that they had sold more tickets than their official capacity allowed. Oldham won the tie 3–1.

Of course, Latics defeat by the only goal of the Littlewoods Final against Notts Forest at Wembley also qualifies.

New Brighton

New Brighton joined the Third Division (North) when it was extended to 22 teams in 1923–24 and narrowly missed promotion the following season when they finished third.

The two clubs first met in 1935–36 when Oldham completed the 'double', winning 6–0 at home and 3–1 at New Brighton. In fact, out of the 18 matches when the two sides met, New Brighton won only three and never won at Boundary Park. Oldham won eight and drew one of the nine matches, scoring 27 goals against seven.

The last season that the two clubs met was 1950–51 after which the New Brighton side lost their League status. In their last season they were top of the table after four games with maximum points!

Newport County

Newport County played more matches than any other ex-member of the Football League.

The Latics first met the Welsh side on 20 August 1962, when the two sides played out a goal-less draw at Somerton Park. Oldham won the return 3–2 and were undefeated in the two other home games that the two sides played. Newport's only success in the six matches that were played was a 2–1 win at home in 1969–70.

The last season that the two sides played was 1970–71 when the Latics were promoted to the Third Division—Oldham winning 4–0 at home and 4–1 at Newport.

Nicknames

Scoring 28 goals in Athletic's first Division Two campaign, Frank Newton (1907–09) rejoiced in the nickname of 'Mary Ann'. The clue given the circumspect style of Edwardian sports reporting was that it was became of 'certain mannerisms on the field of play'.

Perhaps the player with the most unusual nickname was George 'Lady' Woodger (1910–14). His unusual nickname was attributed to his delicate dribbling style, for his nimble feet skipped over the turf like a ballet dancer.

Born ten miles from the Khyber Pass, George 'Cocky' Hunter (1912–13) was an outstanding centre-half. Contemporary reports suggested that Oldham would have won their 1913 semi-final against Aston Villa if they had not transferred Hunter to Chelsea shortly after the third round replay victory at Old Trafford.

A prominent Gaelic footballer 'Sandy' Campbell (1920–24) was noticed by Athletic manager Herbert Bamlett when playing soccer for a BEF team against a French XI in Paris in 1918. Popularly known as 'Tiny', Harry Stafford (1927–34) sustained a leg injury at Southampton in September 1933 which caused his premature retirement from the game.

One player whose nickname defied explanation was Tommy 'Biff' Seymour (1929–36)—a player who was equally at home in either full-back position.

'Spud' Murphy (1929–30) scored on his debut for Athletic but despite this he spent his season in the Reserves unable to dislodge Bill Hasson. Prior to this, the speedy winger had made over 300 appearances for Manchester City and Southampton.

Described as a 'pocket Hercules' Cliff Chadwick (1933–34) proved a very popular player during his short stay at Boundary Park. He was signed following two trail games in the Northern Midweek League team and went straight into the first team, where he scored the winner in a 4–3 victory over Bradford City. Only playing in one league game for Oldham, John Clarke (1937) was dubbed 'the little big-shot' after his scoring debut in a 4–3 win over Barrow. Once described as the 'Durham wonderboy' Kenny Chaytor (1954–60) appeared in the Latics' first team when he was only 16 years old and thus not able to turn professional.

'Big Jim' Bowie (1962–72) was a firm favourite at Boundary Park throughout his ten-years stay. Always cool under pressure, this former inside-forward turned wing-half always tried to use the ball to advantage. Affectionately dubbed 'Road-runner' because of his limitless capacity for action, George Jones (1973–76) joined Athletic as a replacement for David Shaw when the latter joined West Bromwich Albion. Nicknamed 'The Stick' Ian Ormondroyd (1987) showed an unusually deft touch for one so big, but surprisingly despite his height he was not too effective in the air.

Non-League

'Non-League' is the shorthand term for clubs which are not members of the Football League.

Oldham have a fairly good record against non-league clubs in the FA Cup competition, though they have been defeated on two occasions following a drawn first match.

The Latics record is:

Date	Opponents	Venue	Score
28 November 1925	Lytham	Home	10–1
12 December 1925	Stockton	Away	6–4
30 November 1935	Ferryhill Athletic	Home	6–1
29 November 1947	Lancaster City	Home	6–0
11 December 1948	Walthamstow Avenue	Away	2–2
18 December 1948	Walthamstow Avenue	Home	3–1
26 November 1949	Stockton	Home	4–0
24 November 1951	Nelson	Away	4–0
22 November 1952	Boston United	Away	2–1
15 November 1958	Denaby United	Away	2–0
6 December 1958	South Shields	Home	2–0
14 November 1959	Shildon	Away	1–1
17 November 1959	Shildon	Home	3–0
5 November 1960	Rhyl	Away	1–0
4 November 1961	Shildon	Home	5–2
14 November 1964	Hereford United	Home	4–0
2 December 1964	Crook Town	Away	1–0
7 January 1967	Grantham	Away	4–0
15 November 1969	Grantham	Home	3–1
6 December 1969	South Shields	Away	0–0
9 December 1969	South Shields	Home	1–2
18 November 1972	Scarborough	Home	1–1
22 November 1972	Scarborough	Away	1–2
24 November 1972	Formby	Away	2–0
29 January 1977	Northwich Victoria	at Maine Road	3–1

Oldham County

It was in September 1895 that Oldham's first professional soccer club, Oldham County, made an attempt to introduce soccer to the rugby-

playing region—a friendly against Everton. The 4,000 spectators were bemused by soccer's rules and some early reporters wrote of 25-yard lines and conversions!

One season in the Lancashire Combination was followed by two in the Lancashire League. It was in November 1897 during the last of these campaigns that Oldham County failed to fulfil a Lancashire League fixture against Bacup.

Following a meeting of creditors at the Willow Bank Inn, County were forced to retire from the League after only nine games.

Own Goals

In a Second Divison match against Manchester United on 6 October 1923, Sam Wynne had the unusual experience of scoring two goals (one penalty) for his own side and *two* own-goals for United.

As things turned out it wasn't too disastrous, as Latics won 3–2!

Roger Palmer

Roger Palmer beat the Oldham Athletic club scoring record when he hit the target in the club's 4–0 win over Ipswich Town on 4 April 1989. It was his 111th League goal for the Latics, beating the achievements of Eric Gemmell who scored 110 goals between 1947 and 1954. Gemmell in fact, scored 121 goals in all competitve games, compared to Roger Palmer's 155.

One of the club's best-ever buys, Roger has give the Latics splendid service since joining them from Manchester City for £70,000 in November 1980. He has on two occasions finished top scorer, though he has also played quite a lot of his football in midfield.

He started as a Manchester City apprentice, getting his chance in League Football during 1977–78. Though he started only four games, he scored three times.

 Roger Palmer—one of the club's best-ever buys, he holds the club's goalscoring record.

Roger maintained a fine scoring ratio over the few games he played in City's senior side but he could see that his chances at Maine Road were going to be limited, so he readily agreed to move on to Oldham.

In 1982–83 he formed a productive striking partnership with Rodger Wylde, scoring 15 times himself—four short of Wylde's tally. The following season, Roger led the Latics' list with 14 goals. After that, he played in midfield for a while but in 1986–87 he came out on top of the pile again with 17 goals.

In 1987–88, he ran up a total of 20 goals that included hat-tricks against Shrewsbury and Stoke in the Second Division and Carlisle in the Littlewoods Cup.

But the three-goal hit which gave him the most satisfaction came during the early weeks of the 1988–89 season. Roger travelled with Oldham to face his former club, Manchester City, at Maine Road. Just as a reminder as to what he might have done for City, Roger scored three times as Oldham won 4–1.

Penalties

It was Frank Newton who converted the first one received in Latics' opening season in the Football League in the 2–0 home win over Grimsby Town on 16 November 1907.

When Latics played Kidderminster in an FA Cup tie in 1906–7, the referee awarded a penalty against them. The official placed the ball on the spot and then turned round to find there was no goalkeeper. Latics' keeper Bob Hewitson was behind the goal among the fans laying the odds that they would not score—and they didn't, Latics winning 5–0.

Restricted by the brilliance of Jack Hacking at Boundary Park, John Prince made only one appearance in goal in the Football League for Latics. For Northwich Victoria he saved 11 out of 12 penalty kicks awarded against his side.

In 1951–52, the Latics had four successful and different penalty takers—Hardwick, Warner, Gemmell and McKennan.

The scorer of the most penalties for the Latics is Maurice Whittle, who scored from the spot on 18 occasions in the Football League, including 7 in the Latics successful 1973–74 campaign.

In the semi-final of the Anglo-Scottish Cup at St Mirren in October 1978 Latics prevailed 4–2 after spot-kicks, following an extra-time score of 1–1.

Pine Villa

The first time that Pine Villa's name appears in print is Monday 18 November 1895 when the result of the previous Saturday's match reads Pine Villa 4 Boothill Albion 'A' 0.

The Villa was almost certainly chosen in admiration of Aston Villa who had won the League and FA Cup 'double' that same year.

Pine Villa's first ground was located just to the west of Oldham town centre at Berry's Field which was situated to the rear of the Methodist Chapel in Garforth Street, Chadderton. For dressing-rooms, a Smithy close to the Featherstall and Junction Hotel was used. The 'ground' was no more than just one of two unenclosed pitches and before long an alternative venue was obtained.

A suitable piece of land at the side of the Pine Cotton Mill was found and rented.

Pine Villa chose the Oldham Junior League Division Two for their season in 1897–98. Two successful years followed during which time they were promoted, and then finished as runners-up in the First Division to Greenacres.

In July 1899, Pine Villa took over Oldham County's old ground and were on their way to Oldham Athletic.

Play-Offs

Promotion and relegation play-offs were introduced in 1986–87 involving all four divisions. They were used, in part, to reduce the First Division to 20 clubs over two seasons.

In that first season the new promotion play-off formula meant that the top two clubs automatically went up with the next three joining the First Division's representative in an end-of-season knock-out.

Never out of the top three all season, the Latics had to settle for a play-off place when in any other year they would have been promoted automatically. Third played fourth and fifth (Ipswich Town) played

19th in the First Division (Charlton) before the winners met in a play-off final.

Oldham finished seven points ahead of Leeds and in the first leg at Elland Road had held their own until the last minute, when substitute Keith Edwards scored what was to be his first killer goal.

Setting off in the second-leg at Boundary Park with a 1–0 deficit, the Latics levelled matters in the 18th minute when Gary Williams got the final touch to an Ian Ormondroyd header. Oldham pushed forward to seek the First Division status the Club had lost 64 years previously.

The fans were cheering wildly, when with just 90 second to play, teenage substitute Michele Cecere sent a superb header into the Leeds net to put Oldham 2–0 up on the night and 2–1 on aggregate.

However, in a dramatic finale, Leeds stormed forward and substitute Edwards scored his second killer goal to give Leeds the tie on the away-goals rule.

It meant that within a few days, Keith Edwards had twice come on as substitute and twice scored last-minute goals!

Points

Under the three points for a win system which was introduced in 1981–82, the Latics' *best points tally* is the 88 points gained in 1990–91 when the club won the Second Division Championship.

The club's *best points haul* under the old two points for a win system was 62 points from 46 matches in 1973–74, when the Third Divison Championship was won by Latics.

The *worst* record under either system was the meagre 25 points secured in 1953–54 when the club was relegated to the Third Division (North).

Premier League

With just six weeks of the first FA Premier League season to go, Latics fans must have given up all hope of seeing their side survive the inevitable—relegation.

The club were ensconced at the foot of the table, a point behind Notts Forest and another adrift of Middlesbrough.

But there was a remarkable recovery—a 3–2 home win over Liverpool on a cold, unwelcoming evening and a 1–0 victory over Manchester United to throw a spanner albeit a temporarily into the Championship race. Even so, the run-in threw up the prospect of Oldham having to win at Aston Villa and at home to Southampton.

A Nicky Henry goal at Villa Park provided the Latics with unexpected momentum and United their first title for 26 years.

The final game at home to Southampton required a conclusive victory in the hope that Crystal Palace would not get any form of a result against London rivals Arsenal.

In a bizarre afternoon of footballing action, Latics plundered an astonishing victory over the Saints with goals from Pointon, Olney, Ritchie and Halle as Palace went down 2–0 at Highbury.

Level on points with Palace, the Latics remained in the Premier League by virtue of a superior goal difference!

In 1993–94, the Latics finally lost their desperate fight for Premier League survival despite a gutsy final fling at Carrow Road. The Latics were virtually doomed before the kick-off following the four-games-in-eight days schedule, which would have tested the strongest squad in the Premiership. For Oldham, with five senior players out with injuries, it became a burden they found difficult to bear.

There is no doubt that the turning point in Oldham's topsy-turvy season was the last-minute Mark Hughes equaliser in the FA Cup semi-final. The danger signs were there when West Ham United won at Boundary Park on 16 April straight after the semi-final setback. That dropped Oldham back in the bottom three after they had been climbing just before their two ties with United. Tottenham's 2–0 win on 5 May was a killer, but the draws with both Sheffield clubs had left the Latics struggling on their sandy, strength-sapping pitch.

On the last Saturday of the season the miracle Joe Royle's men needed to stay in the top flight just did not materialise, and so the Latics lost their brave battle to stay in the Premiership.

The club's record in the Premier League is:

P	W	D	L	F	A
84	22	23	39	105	142

Programme Monthly

In 1983–84, Programme Monthly—the leading magazine for programme collectors—announced that the Latics' publication came top of the list for the Second Division "Best Cover Design". It was the first award ever won by the Athletic Matchday Magazine.

The original idea for the design came from Commercial Manager Alan Hardy, who then asked the Oldham Evening Chronicle to supply a colour action photograph.

Promotion

The Latics have won promotion six times. In 1909–10, the club won 14 of their last 16 matches to earn promotion to the First Division on goal average. Manchester City were champions, whilst Oldham were one of three teams to finish on 53 points. The Latics goal average (2.03) was better than that of Hull City (1.74) and Derby County (1.53). The last two matches of the season were the key ones when home victories over their nearest rivals, Hull City (3–0) and Derby County (4–0) were chalked up. Just how close the finish to the race for promotion had been can be judged from the final figures of the leading teams:

	P	W	D	L	F	A	Pts
Manchester City	38	23	8	7	81	40	54
Oldham Athletic	38	23	7	8	79	39	53
Hull City	38	23	7	8	80	46	53
Derby County	38	22	9	7	72	47	53

After relegation to the Second Division in 1922–23 and the Third Division North in 1934–35, the Latics next won promotion in 1952–53. The championship was in doubt until the last match, where a goal-less draw at Bradford City ensured that the Latics finished a point ahead of Port Vale who had the better goal average. It was a highly entertaining campaign when only one team went up, but Latics were worthy champions:

	P	W	D	L	F	A	Pts
Oldham Athletic	46	22	15	9	77	45	59
Port Vale	46	20	18	8	67	35	58

There then followed another relegation after just one season in Division Two, and in 1957–58 the lower 12 clubs of Divisions Three (North and South) formed the new Division Four.

It had to be "promotion or bust" in 1962–63 according to Frank Armitage, the club chairman. Yet it turned out to be promotion and bust-up! Though the Latics finished as runners-up, beating Southport 11–0 on Boxing Day, behind the scenes a row had been simmering which ended with the board voting 6–4 to ask for manager Jack Rowley's resignation.

	P	W	D	L	F	A	Pts
Brentford	46	27	8	11	98	64	62
Oldham Athletic	46	24	11	11	95	60	59
Crewe Alexandra	46	24	11	11	86	58	59
Mansfield Town	46	24	9	13	108	69	57
Gillingham	46	22	13	11	71	49	57

After six seasons in the Third Division the club were relegated to the Fourth Division in 1968–69, but in 1970–71 the Latics won promotion for the second time in nine seasons. A disastrous run in March threatened to cost the club its chance and the closing weeks of the campaign became quite tense. A goal-less draw at Workington on 24 April clinched the move to the Third Division:

	P	W	D	L	F	A	Pts
Notts County	46	30	9	7	89	36	69
Bournemouth	46	24	12	10	81	46	60
Oldham Athletic	46	24	11	11	88	63	59
York City	46	23	10	13	78	54	56
Chester	46	24	7	15	69	55	55

In 1973–74 the Latics won the Third Division championship, the club's success being largely due to a breath-taking series of wins close to the end of the season. A run of ten successive wins from 12 January to 12 March followed three weeks later by a run of seven undefeated games, in which only one point was dropped, saw the club chasing the divisonal championship. With two games remaining, the Latics needed one point to win the championship and two to keep out York City whose goal-average was inferior to Oldhams. The Latics lost 2–0 at home to Charlton, but in the last game a goal-less draw at Plymouth sealed the title:

	P	W	D	L	F	A	Pts
Oldham Athletic	46	25	12	9	83	47	62
Bristol Rovers	46	22	17	7	65	33	61
York City	46	21	19	6	67	38	61
Wrexham	46	22	12	12	63	43	56

The last time the Latics figured in a successful promotion campaign was in 1990–91. They started the season in splendid form with five straight wins and were undefeated until the 17th game when they went down 1–0 to Port Vale.

Only eight defeats in 46 League games underlined the consistency of the Latics. The club's final game of the season saw them beat arch rivals Sheffield Wednesday 3–2 with Neil Redfearn slotting home a 90th minute penalty to send Latics' fans wild.

	P	W	D	L	F	A	Pts
Oldham Athletic	46	25	13	8	83	53	88
West Ham United	46	24	15	7	60	34	87
Sheffield Wednesday	46	22	16	8	80	51	82
Notts County	46	23	11	12	76	55	80

Re-election

In 1955–56, seven points from their last six games had saved the Latics from having to apply for re-election for the first time in their history, but in 1958–59 they finished the season in the bottom four of Division Four and had to apply for re-election.

However, Latics worst experience came in 1959–60 when the club finished second from bottom of the Fourth Division and had to seek re-election for the second successive season. Only Hartlepool United were below them.

Relegation

The Latics have on four occasions experienced the anguish of relegation. For four post-war seasons the club retained First Division status, though they were always within sight of the relegation zone. They were relegated for the first time in the club's history in 1922–23 when they finished bottom of the First Division. Halfway through the campaign, team boss Charlie Roberts resigned and David Ashworth was asked to return to see if his old magic would save the Latics from the drop, but unfortunately "too late" was the cry.

In 1934–35, the Latics were relegated from the Second Division and forced to make their debut the following season in Division Three North. Their away form in 1934–35 had seen them draw three and lose 18 of their 21 games. A sign of the time was the loss of manager Jimmy McMullan without replacement.

After winning the Division Three North championship in 1952–53, the following season saw the Latics finish bottom of Division Two. Manager Hardwick tried to rely on virtually the same players that had won promotion, and although the team drew 4–4 at Luton on the opening day of the season, they went eight matches without a win to end the campaign with only eight wins and a mere 25 points.

In 1968–69 after six seasons in the Third Division, the Latics were relegated to the Fourth Division for the first time in their history, though they had a 5 year spell there from 1957–68 when the regionalised Third Divisions merged. The club went from bad to worse and by the end of November Jack Rowley had returned as manager. Things improved slightly under Jimmy Frizzell's coaching, but a spate of injuries towards the end of the season killed off Latics' hopes and they were relegated.

Rhodesia

During the Latics 1967 tour of Rhodesia and Malawi, local witch doctors were reported to have spread voodo powers among the home teams goal lines to prevent Oldham scoring. It was not successful as Athletic scored 45 goals in 11 games, only one of which was lost!

v St Paul's (Rhodesia National Champions	Won	6–0
v Rio Tinto	Lost	2–3
v F.A.R. XI (Football Association of Rhodesia)	Won	3–1
v Dynamos (National League North Zone Leaders)	Won	4–2
v Mangula	Won	4–0
v Great Dykes Association XI	Won	7–3
v Tornados	Won	3–2

v Manicaland XI	Won	2–1
v Salisbury Callies	Won	5–2
v Malawi FA	Won	3–2
v Blantyre Sports Club	Won	6–2

Charlie Roberts

Charlie Roberts was one of the greatest centre-halves of his era—a time when those players were attacking players. He had begun his career with Darlington and Grimsby but Manchester United signed him for £400 shortly after the turn of the century. He played for England in all matches against Northern Ireland, Wales and Scotland in 1904–5 and he went on to established himself as a top player with United. It came as a complete surprise to United fans when they allowed him to leave during the 1913 close-season when Oldham stepped in smartly to secure his signature.

He cost Oldham a club record fee, but was worth every penny of the £1,750 they paid. He was a great captain and Latics achieved their best-ever League position under his captaincy when they ended the 1914–15 season one point behind Everton, the League Champions. Sadly, Charlie received a serious injury during the war that finished his playing career.

In July 1921 he was appointed Latics manager, but found the transition to management a difficult task. Only a late burst in the final 11 matches of that 1921–22 season secured 19th place in the first Divison and ensured that relegation was avoided. The club started the 1922–23 campaign with three wins and a draw from the opening five fixtures, but it was too good to last and from 16 September 1922 to 27 January 1923 only two wins were recorded from 22 League games. In the midst of this crisis, Charlie Roberts resigned.

On his death in August 1939, The Manchester Guardian obituary described him as the greatest captain Manchester United and Oldham Athletic ever had. He was also a leading figure in the Players Union dispute of 1909.

"Today" wrote the paper, "the Union flourishes. Roberts became its first chairman and later vice-president and trustee. It is a worthy memorial to a great player and a great sportsman."

Oldham's full league record under Charlie Roberts was:

P	W	D	L	F	A
65	18	16	31	63	94

Jack Rowley

Jack Rowley had two spells as club manager. He first came to Boundary Park in July 1960 after the Latics had survived an application for re-election to the Fourth Division.

After an uncertain start, the 1960–61 season 'took off' in October, the month in which Ken Branagan, Bobby Johnstone and Bert Lister all made their club debuts. He brought about a steady improvement each season and in 1962–63, the Latics won promotion.

As the team celebrated their promotion by beating Hartlepool United 6–1 at Boundary Park, there could have been few among the crowd with any idea of the bombshell which followed three days later. A dispute arose between Rowley and the board and he left as the Latics were still celebrating their success.

He was re-appointed manager in October 1968, inheriting a side at the bottom of Division Three. Despite some improvement in mid-season, relegation was not averted and when the next season started in similar fashion, manager Rowley left for the last time.

He also managed Plymouth Argyle, Ajax, Wrexham and Bradford Park Avenue, but he is probably best remembered for his playing successes.

He was one of the most successful goalscorers of the post-war period, netting a Manchester United record of 182 league goals. His tally for 1951–52 of 30 league goals was then a club record. A reserve player with Wolves, Jack Rowley made his league debut for Bournemouth in 1936–37, but his potential was such that United snapped him up the following season.

Jack Rowley—he had two spells as club manager. As a player, he once scored four times for England in their 9–2 victory over Northern Ireland at Maine Road in 1949.

Jack Rowley replaced Stan Mortensen in the England team against Switzerland in December 1948, but in spite of scoring on his debut appearance, he was dropped! He later took his cap total to six and

scored four times in England's 9–2 victory over Northern Ireland at Maine Road in 1949.

United's top scorer in the first four post-war seasons, he won a richly deserved League Championship medal in 1952. He also scored twice at Wembley when they defeated Blackpool 4–2 in the 1948 FA Cup final.

Oldham's full league record under Jack Rowley was:

P	W	D	L	F	A
196	76	44	76	324	321

Royal Visit

On Wednesday 6 July 1921, HRH The Prince of Wales visited Boundary Park and drew one of the best crowds ever seen at the ground!

The terraces were crammed with more than 40,000 ex-servicemen, disabled soldiers, factory workers and school children. Streamers of coloured buntings added to the scene and even the old Press box had a fresh coat of green paint for the occasion. In the centre of the ground, a special low stand was erected for The Prince to receive the presentees.

Joe Royle

Joe Royle first arrived on the Everton scene in 1966 when Harry Catterick put a fresh-faced 16-year old from Norris Green into a First Division match against Blackpool.

He played in two games that season and four more the next, scoring three goals to indicate that Everton had unearthed a centre-forward who would follow in the line established by the likes of Dixie Dean and Tommy Lawton.

In 1967 he was established in a new-look side that tacked on to the triumphs in the era of Alex Young. Joe scored 64 goals in 122 League games to the time the championship was won in 1970. Yet he had to

Joe Royle—current Oldham manager. A manager who is able to get the best out of his players.

wait until 1971 for his first England cap in a friendly in Malta. He played his last game for Norwich City in December 1981 and eventually retired because of a knee injury after 15 years in League football.

Joe was appointed Oldham's manager on 14 July 1982, arriving at Boundary Park on the back of a lorry!

On his way to the ground to meet local and national press men, he had to hitch a lift after his car broke down on the M62 motorway. "My first job as manager will be to get a reliable car" said Royle—a sense of humour that was to stand him in good stead for the future!

Success was not achieved overnight and Oldham had to ward off tempting offers from Manchester City for their enthusiastic boss, but in the late 80s Oldham Athletic established themselves in the national game. The events of season 1989–90 were incredible. They nearly won three titles, but ended with nothing. They just missed out on promotion from Division Two, lost at Wembley to Notts Forest in the Final of the Littlewoods Cup, then to Manchester United in the replayed FA Cup semi-final.

Joe eventually led his team into Division One in May 1991—and it was a testament to his ability to get the best out of his players and to his faith in attacking football.

Though at the end of the 1993–94 season the Latics lost their fight to stay in the Premiership, Joe Royle signed a new three-year deal!

Oldham's full league record under Joe Royle is:

P	W	D	L	F	A
518	190	144	184	755	747

Rugby League

On Sunday 10 January 1982 the Latics and Oldham Rugby League Club, who were both bidding for promotion, joined forces to create local sporting history.

With the Rugby Club's Watersheddings Ground frost bound, their 'Home' game against Yorkshire rivals Batley took place at Boundary Park, where the pitch was protected by undersoil heating. The result, a victory for Oldham by 17–9 in the first ever Rugby League match at Boundary Park.

Second Division

Starting their Football League career in the Second Division in 1907–8, the Latics three seasons in that League saw them lose only three home games. In that first season, the Latics finished third and came so close to becoming the first side in history to win promotion to the First Divison in one season of League football.

Though the Latics' second season in Division Two was bitterly disappointing, they won 14 of the last 16 end-of-the-season performances in 1909–10 and earned promotion to Division One on goal average.

The club were relegated for the first time in their history in 1923. In 1924–25 there was panic in the Oldham camp which lasted until the final game of the season which saw Latics win 1–0 at Crystal Palace. It was Jack Keedwell's goal that ensured the Latics stayed up while Palace went down with Coventry City.

In 1929–30 defeat at Barnsley 1–2 in the last game of the season left the Latics in third place, whereas a win would have sealed the club's return to Division One. Relegation arrived in 1934–35, Latics' away form which produced 18 defeats and 3 draws in 21 games deserved little else.

Returning to the Second Division and Third Division (North) Champions, the Latics spent only one season back in the higher

Division as George Hardwick relied virtually on the same players that had gained the club promotion. Although the team drew 4–4 at Luton on the opening day of the season, they went eight matches without a win and ended the campaign bottom of Division Two.

In winning the Third Division Championship, the Latics returned to the Second Division for a fourth spell, but from late-October onwards they were concerned about dropping straignt down.

The club had another relegation scare in 1978–79 but the last six home games were won and Latics climbed to a respectable position.

The club's new manager, Joe Royle, soon established himself and in 1982–83 chased for promotion but then flirted with relegation the next.

In 1986–87, the club finished third and had they done so in any recent campaign they would have been promoted, but this was the season the play-offs were introduced. There were never any doubts that Oldham would not achieve their aim. Seven defeats in 44 League games underlined the Latics consistency as they lifted the Second Division Championship. The club's last game in May 1991 saw Neil Redfern score from the penalty spot in the last minute of the game with Sheffield Wednesday to secure a 3–2 victory.

The club's record in the Second Division is:

P	W	D	L	F	A
1388	521	356	511	1995	2019

Secretaries

Tom Smyth was appointed Oldham Athletic's club secretary on 1 March 1973 and resigned two days later because of ill-health, making him the shortest serving club secretary in Football League history.

Semi-finals

The Latics first semi-final appearance came in 1913–14 when they went down by the only goal of the game to Aston Villa at Blackburn. Though the venue favoured Oldham, their opponents had already won the FA Cup four times and were in their eighth semi-final.

The crowd of 22,616 meant that the ground was only half full and this detracted somewhat from the normal atmosphere of a semi-final.

The goal came after 32 minutes, when Stephenson met Wallace's cross and he scored with a low shot which beat Matthews comfortably. The Athletic pressed hard in the second half with Woodger coming closest, but Hardy dived at the foot of the post to make a good save.

The club's second appearance in a semi-final came in the two-legged Littlewoods Cup competition of 1989–90. Drawn against First Division West Ham, the Latics rewrote the club's then 95-year-old record books. A devastating display saw them beat the Hammers 6–0 in the first leg at Boundary Park. The floodgates opened as early as the 11th minute when Neil Adams slammed home a superb 20-yard drive off the post. Andy Ritchie and Earl Barratt added further goals before half-time and if West Ham entertained any thoughts of sneaking back into the contest in the second half, they were rudely shattered within 30 seconds after the interval when Rick Holden lashed home a fourth. Further goals from Ritchie and Palmer completed the rout.

Though there were some anxious moments in the second leg at Upton Park as Latics lost 3–0, there was no denying that Oldham were the better side over two legs.

Also in that never to be forgotten 1989–90 season, the Latics appeared in the FA Cup semi-finals for the first time in 77 years. Drawn against Manchester United, they suffered the narrowest of defeats after two epic encounters.

The first match had so many twists and turns—Earl Barratt putting Latics ahead after only six minutes; though goals from Robson and Webb took United into the lead, a cracking first-time right-foot volley from Ian Marshall levelled the scores. The game went into extra-time and when Danny Wallace put the Reds ahead it looked like the end of the road for the Latics, but substitute Roger Palmer ghosted in at the far post to meet Marshall's cross and take the game to a replay.

The club's dreams of an amazing Wembley double were shattered in the second match at Maine Road by Mark Robins, a Chadderton lad who played for Boundary Park Juniors.

Brian McClair gave United the lead, but Andy Ritchie levelled things up to take the game into extra-time once again. It was in the 110th minute that Robins sneaked a low shot past Hallworth in the Oldham goal, though he might have been offside!

In two splendid matches, it was impossible for the impartial observer to say which was the First Division team.

Last season, Latics reached a semi-final for the fourth time and once again Manchester United were the opponents.

After 90 minutes the FA Cup semi-final played at Wembley on Sunday 10 April was goal-less, but in extra-time Neil Pointon gave Oldham the lead. Only seconds remained when Mark Hughes crashed home a superb equaliser to take the semi-final tie to a second match.

The replay at Maine Road three days later saw a rampant United beat the Latics 4–1 with Neil Pointon again grabbing the Oldham goal.

David Shaw

David Shaw had a splendid career in League Football. It lasted a good twelve seasons from 1966 to 1978, when he was forced to quit the game with a knee injury. During that time he scored a total of 109 goals in 323 appearances, including 90 in two spells for the Latics.

After leaving school, he joined Huddersfield Town as a junior and turned professional at Leeds Road in January 1967. A clash of heads saw David burst an artery and put him in hospital for repairs. Discharged, he took up his career again, but the wound opened up to send him back into hospital for further surgery. After eight weeks of treatment, he returned to action only to suffer severe cartilage damage almost immediately and be forced to return to hospital.

But in September 1969 with his career at a low ebb, he joined Oldham Athletic for a fee of £40,000.

His impact with Athletic was devastating. He became a big favourite with the fans at Boundary Park and helped Oldham win promotion from the Third Division in 1970–71. He was at his peak that season.

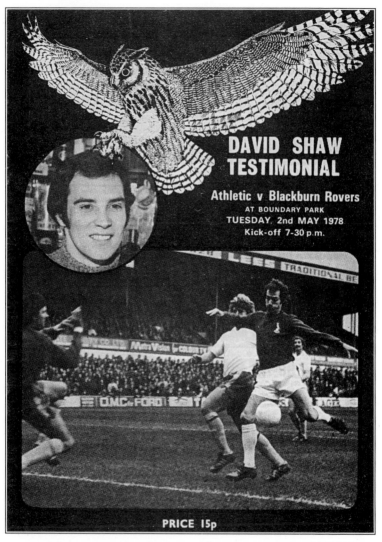

DAVID SHAW TESTIMONIAL

Athletic v Blackburn Rovers
AT BOUNDARY PARK
TUESDAY, 2nd MAY 1978
Kick-off 7-30 p.m.

PRICE 15p

He delighted and thrilled the Oldham fans, crashing in 24 goals, many of them spectacular. Some of them defied description for their power and for the sudden quality of unexpectedness they brought to the game.

One of the best kept secrets of that time was that David Shaw nearly enrolled in Bill Shankley's soccer academy at Liverpool. 'Shanks'

would go into raptures when talking about David Shaw's potential, but decided to look elsewhere when he was informed that David was a trifle short-sighted.

But the First Division was still calling and in March 1973 he joined West Bromwich Albion for £77,000, after he had accrued an excellent League record with the Latics: 69 goals in 155 outings, including a hat-trick against Southampton in 12 minutes!

He never really settled with the Albion and though he scored 20 goals in 96 first team appearances, he was in fact nicknamed 'super sub' and netted quite a few important goals after joining the fray in the No. 12 shirt.

He returned to Boundary Park in December 1975 on a free transfer because the accumulation of knocks he had taken over the years had finally resulted in a

David Shaw—one of the most popular Latic players during his two spells with the club.

serious knee injury.

He was to play another vital role in consolidating the Latics in the Second Division—scoring a further 21 goals in 55 games.

Without the knee injury and an accumulation of years of fierce competition where the pressure is at its worst, David Shaw would have gone on scoring goals and delighting crowds for several more years.

Silver Spade

In July 1896 when the Mayor of Oldham, Alderman Thomas Bolton, cut the first sod on Boundary Park, he was presented with a specially engraved silver spade to mark the occasion.

For over 50 years afterwards, the whereabouts of the spade was shrouded in mystery, but in 1948 Percy Skipworth, then the longest-serving member of the Oldham board of directors heard that the implement had been 'rediscovered'. For sentimental reasons, Mr and Mrs Skipworth decided to purchase the spade and present it to the Club so that it would be displayed in the Boundary Park boardroom.

The spade has a solid silver blade and an ebony handle and shaft encircled by two silver bands. The Oldham coat-of-arms are engraved on the blade together with an inscription noting the circumstances in which it was presented to Alderman Bolton.

Simod Cup

A crowd of 1,841, the competitions lowest ever, watched Oldham's only game in the Simod Cup which replaced the Full Members' Cup for the 1987–88 season.

West Bromwich Albion were the visitors. The Throstles winning 3–0 against what was a very poor Latics display.

Southport

Southport's League career lasted from 1921–22, when they were founder members of the Third Division (North) until they failed to gain re-election in 1977–78 when they lost their place to Wigan Athletic on a second Ballot.

Bert Lister—one of Latics' most prolific centre-forwards. He scored six goals in Oldham's 11–0 win over Southport in 1962.

The clubs first met in the Football League in season 1935–36 when a Fred Leedham goal earned Latics a point at Southport. The return fixture saw Oldham triumph 4–0. In 1946–47 both sides won the away fixture by 4–2, whilst two seasons later Oldham completed the first of four 'doubles' over Southport.

On Boxing Day 1962 the Latics produced a brilliant team effort against lowly Southport, equalling the club record of 11 goals in a game. On a snow-covered pitch, Athletic led by nine goals as early as the 53rd minute and there was hope that they would smash the club record. Although Bobby Johnstone was the architect of the victory, the limelight fell on Bert Lister who scored six goals.

The size of the win was a record for the Fourth Division and Southport's biggest defeat.

The two clubs last met in season 1973–74 with Latics winning both matches, 2–0 at Southport and 6–0 at Boundary Park, where Colin Garwood grabbed at hat-trick.

Sporting Latics

Wilkin Ward (1906–8) joined Athletic in their pre-league days. A versatile sportsman, he was a professional runner as well as a footballer and played as a win-threequarter for Rochdale Hornets.

Bill Appleyard (1908) a prolific goalscorer in the Newcastle United side of the Edwardian era, made 4 appearances for Athletic. He was a good billiards player and appeared in several exhibition games in the Oldham district.

A centre-forward who main assets were a blistering turn of pace and total commitment over the ninety minutes, Fred Broadbent (1920–1923) won many trophies on the running track. At Broughton Rangers RFC ground, he received five yards in a 60-yard dash against the British champion, W. R. Applegarth and won by two yards.

Howard Baker's (1929) only appearance for Latics came in 1928–29 when he deputised for Jack Hacking. Baker was the British high-jump champion and represented England in the 1912 and 1920 Olympic Games. He was also an outstanding high-diver, water-polo goalkeeper and lawn tennis player.

Another player only the represent the Latics on one occasion was Bill Baldwin (1933) who in 1965, won the All-England Cup for Bowls. Tommy Dryburgh (1957) also played in only one game for the Latics, preferring to play Ice Hockey for the Kirkaldy Fliers.

Reg Blore (1965–1970) was rarely absent from Athletic's first team, following his signing from Blackburn Rovers. In 1968, he was the winner of the Professional Footballers' Golf Championship.

Substitutes

Substitutes were first allowed in the Football League in season 1965–66. The first appearance of a substitute in League football came just down the road at Burnden Park, when Charlton Athletic's Keith Peacock came on during Wanderer's 4–2 win.

Oldham's first substitute was Alan Lawson who came on to replace the injured Albert Jackson (and scored) against Peterborough United at Boundary Park on 28 August 1965, the first day that substitutes were allowed.

The greatest number of substitutes used in a single season by the Latics under the single substitute rule was 31 in 1985–86, but since 1986–87 two substitutes have been allowed and in 1990–91 the club used 67 in the 46 matches.

The greatest number of substitute appearances for the Latics has been made by Roger Palmer who came on during 40 League games.

It was in 1990–91 that Paul Moulden caused us to re-write the Latics records on the matter of substitutes with 13 League appearances in the number 12 shirt.

Sunday Football

The first Sunday games played by first-class clubs was during the power crisis of 1973–74.

The first game ever involved the Latics in a third round FA Cup tie at Cambridge United on the morning of 6 January 1974, when 8,479 spectators saw the clubs draw 2–2. It was Latics' Andy Lochead who scored the first goal in what was the first FA Cup tie to be played on a Sunday.

In 1986–87, Latics were never out of the top three all season but had to settle for a play-off place, when in any other year they would have been promoted automatically. After losing to the only goal of the game at Leeds, the return leg was played on Sunday 17 May 1987 in front of 19,126 spectators. Oldham fans were celebrating wildly, for it was 2–0 on the night and 2–1 on aggregate, but Keith Edwards' goal gave Leeds the tie on the away-goals rule.

The next important match played on a Sunday was the FA Cup semi-final match with Manchester United at Maine Road on 8 April 1990. The clubs fought out a gripping contest which ended all square at 3–3, and though Latics went down 2–1 in the replay they did get to Wembley later that month. In fact, on Sunday 29 April, the town was virtually closed as Latics travelled south for the biggest day in the club's history. Unfortunately, one goal from Nigel Jemson broke Athletic's heart and gave Notts Forest the Littlewoods Cup.

Since then, the club have played several Sunday fixtures with the advent of Sky TV, the most notable perhaps being Latics' 1–0 victory on 2 May 1993 at Aston Villa to thwart their Premier League Championship quest.

Last season the FA Cup semi-final at Wembley between Latics and Manchester United was played on Sunday 10 April, with Neil Pointon scoring for Oldham in 1–1 draw.

Supporters Club

By the mid 1920s the receipts from the "gate" had been steadily dwindling and the directors faced a pile of debts. With attendances continuing to plunge, it was obvious that the club was going to fold unless something could be done.

The Supporters Club founded in 1924 did invaluable work, raising much needed finance through firework displays, jazz band concerts, garden parties, boxing and Christmas draws.

The next decade once again saw Athletic struggling financially. The Supporters Club executive worked wonders but Oldham owed an enormous debt to an anonymous friend of the Supporters Club, who, with wages overdue, lent the money and save an embarrassing collapse.

Suspensions

Athletic's first goalkeeper in the Football League, Bob Hewitson was suspended by the FA following an ill-tempered match against Fulham on 15 February 1908, when he was alleged to have hurled a lump of turf at the referee. Then shortley after returning to Oldham's league team, he was suspended by the Athletic board for insubordination.

Another goalkeeper, Hugh McDonald was an ever-present in 1910–11, Athletic's first season in Division One and continued in the first team the following year, but was dropped and then refused to travel to Everton for a reserve match in September 1911. He was fined, transfer-listed and suspended for a month, before moving to Bradford.

Billy Cook was suspended for 12 months from 16 April 1915 after being sent-off at Middlesbrough and refusing to leave the field. Bob Stewart's robust style did not always find favour with referees and he

was suspended for two months after being sent-off against Arsenal on 7 February 1920.

Tommy Davis proved an excellent capture for the Latics, yet he began his Boundary Park career with a three-month suspension after breaking his contract with a French club to sign for Oldham.

Sustained Scoring

In Latics' first Football League campaign, Frank Newton netted 28 goals in 36 matches, including a spell of 8 goals in 7 matches. John Blair's outstanding form in 1923–24 when he scored 14 goals in 17 appearances was curtailed by a serious leg injury.

Following his signing from Port Vale in January 1929, Stewart Littlewood's 12 goals in 18 appearances was an important element in the club's escape from relegation at the end of that season. The following season, he did even better with 26 goals in 38 matches.

Bill Johnstone arrived at Boundary Park in January 1931 and made an immediate impact with 13 goals in his first 16 games.

In 1936–37, Tommy Davis established the Oldham record for the number of goals scored in a league season with 33 from 39 matches, including 10 goals in a six-match spell at the beginning of the season.

Eric Sykes

It was in November 1975 that comedian Eric Sykes accepted an invitation to join the Oldham Athletic Board.

A noted script-writer and a star of stage, films and television, Eric Syke's association with the Latics goes back to his school-days when he lived in Ward Street and attended the local school.

Shortly after his appointment to the Board, it was evident that he retained fond memories of seeing Athletic in action. Yet twenty-one months later he resigned from the Oldham Board. Due to outside pressures of work he felt he couldn't justify his position.

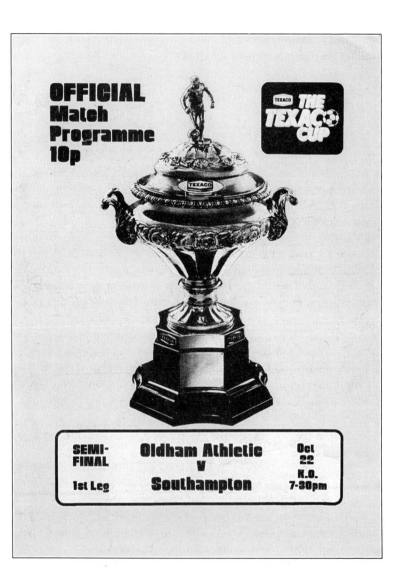

Texaco Cup

The predecessor of the Anglo-Scottish Cup, it was launched in 1970–71 and was for English, Irish and Scottish club sides not involved in European competitions that season.

The Texaco Cup provided Latics fans with some tremendous moments to remember and in 1974–75, the last season of the competition, the club progressed to the semi-final stages, where they went down over two legs to Southampton.

Third Division

The Latics were relegated to the Third Division (North) for the first time in their history.at the end of the 1934–35 season, when they finished next to the bottom of the Second Division with 26 points.

The club's first season in the lower division saw them finish seventh on 45 points with Bill Walsh scoring a record 32 goals. That first season in the Third Division (North) saw them lose 13–4 to Tranmere Rovers on Boxing Day, which remains the club's worst league defeat. The Latics spent eleven seasons either side of the Second World War in the Third Division before winning the Championship and promotion to Division Two in 1952–53.

Unfortunately, the Latics only spent one season in the Second Division and with a mere 25 points returned to the Third Division. In 1957–58 12 clubs from the Third Division (North) were to drop out into a Fourth Division and when the season ended Latics finished 15th and were founder members of the Fourth Division.

The next two seasons saw the club finish in the bottom four of Divison Four and having to apply for re-election, but in 1962–63 the Latics finished the season as runners-up to Brentford and were back in the Third Division.

The club's third spell in this Division saw them spend six seasons before returning to Division Four in 1968–69 when they finished bottom. After just two seasons in soccer's basement, the club returned

 Members of the Latics squad which won the Third Division Chapionship in 1973–74.

to Division Three for the 1971–72 season and in 1973–74 won the Third Division Championship with a record 62 points (under the two points for a win system) sealing it with a goalless draw at Plymouth. The club collected 30 away points—a record for the national Third Division.

The club's full record in the Third Division is:

P	W	D	L	F	A
1072	402	267	393	1678	1611

Throw-ins

Ryszard Kowenicki's game featured quite a remarkable throwing-in technique, the follow-through of which occasionally left him nose-downwards on the field, yet with his toes still grounded behind the touchline!

Perhaps the Latics player with the longest throw-in was Albert Watson, reminiscent of Sammy Weaver, the best-known pre-war exponent of that art.

Transfers

Signed from Manchester United on 26 August 1913 for a then club record fee of £1,750, Charlie Roberts led Athletic to their best-ever League position when they ended the 1914–15 season one point adrift of Everton. Another player who cost Latics their record transfer fee was Jim Marshall who joined the club from Bradford City on 23 September 1920 for £2,250.

A typical piece of Oldham business was the capture of Simon Stainrod. Signed from Sheffield United for a club record fee of £60,000, he was transferred some twenty months later to Queen's Park Rangers for £250,000.

Kenny Clements cost Latics £200,000 (a club record fee) when he joined them from Manchester City on 13 September 1979. A firm favourite at Boundary Park, he displayed many clever touches for a player who was so obviously 'one-footed'.

A bargain buy from Leeds United in January 1986, Andy Linighan realised Latics incoming fee (£350,000) when he left for Norwich City in March 1988.

When Mike Milligan joined Everton on 24 August 1990, he became Athletic's first ever £1 million sale, and with the club's finances more buoyant than perhaps at any other time in their history the Latics' transfer record was broken three times in quick succession. John Keeley (£240,000 from Brighton), David Currie (£450,000 from Notts Forest) and Richard Jobson (£460,000 from Hull City) were all brought in.

In February 1992, Earl Barratt signed for Aston Villa for £1.7 million, thus realising the club's record incoming fee, whilst some seven months later, Ian Olney made the reverse journey for £700,000, Latics' costliest signing.

Undefeated

Oldham Athletic have remained undefeated at home in just one League season and that was the club's initial season in 1907–8.

The club's best and longest undefeated home sequence in the Football League is of 26 matches between 20 February 1937 and 7 May 1938.

The Latics longest run of undefeated Football League matches, home and away, is 15 between 15 September 1937 and 15 January 1938.

Undersoil Heating

It was in 1980 that Oldham Athletic joined the select band of clubs to install undersoil heating on the pitch.

With the help of local business sponsorship and lottery money, work was able to get underway in mid-May.

The "Meltaway" under-pitch soilwarming system was installed by a Swedish company at a cost of £60,000. Operating from an oil-fired boiler, 16 miles of plastic cable under the playing area circulated water at a temperature of 20°c to prevent the surface freezing over in winter.

The system was completed and ready for use in December 1980 and was used for the first time for the match against Grimsby Town on 27 December which Latics lost 2–1.

It was a £60,000 investment that proved its worth on only a limited number of occasions. When the plastic pitch was installed in 1985, the undersoil heating was removed.

 Work starts on the undersoil heating in 1980, and was first used on 27th December 1980 against Grimsby Town.

Utility Players

A utility player is one of those particularly gifted footballers who can play in different positions.

One of the best utility players ever to represent Oldham was Matt Gray, who cost nothing more than a £10 signing-on fee and gave many

years of splendid service. Initially, he played in the forward line, but later moved to centre-half.

Another player to prove his all-round ability was Lewis Brook. Signed from Huddersfield Town as a centre-forward, he scored seven goals in 11 appearances during the later stages of the 1947–48 season. In subsequent campaigns he appeared in all but one of the outfield positions, eventually making a splendid full-back partner to George Hardwick.

Jimmy Frizzell was originally an inside-forward, though he was at home in almost every position, and like Lewis Brook, wore every outfield shirt except one. He was the club's leading goalscorer in seasons 1961–62 and 1964–65, before being successfully converted to wing-half and later still to full-back.

Towards the ends of the 1960s, players were encouraged to become more adaptable and to see their role as less stereotyped. At the same time however, much less attention came to be paid to the implication of wearing a certain numbered shirt and accordingly, some of the more versatile players came to wear almost all the different numbered shirts at some stage or another, although this did not necessarily indicate a vast variety of positions.

Darron McDonough, who was one of the most whole-hearted players ever to pull on an Oldham shirt, wore every outfield shirt except number 3. He was an almost automatic choice by virtue of his 100% displays in whatever position he was chosen.

Victories

In a Season

The Latics greatest number of victories in a season in 25 in 1973–74, which included 12 away wins, another record.

In a Match

Latics best victories in the major competitions are as follows:

Home

Football League	11–0	*v.* Southport	1962–63
FA Cup	10–1	*v.* Lytham	1925–26
Football League Cup	7–0	*v.* Scarborough	1989–90

Away

Football League	6–0	*v.* Darlington	1947–48
FA Cup	6–4	*v.* Stockton	1925–26
Football League Cup	3–1	*v.* Bury	1970–71
		v. Workington	1975–76

These results are since the club's admission to the Football League, though prior to that Latics beat Parkfield Central 13–1 in the Manchester Junior Cup First Round match on 30 January 1904.

Wartime Football

First World War

In spite of the outbreak of war in 1914, the major football leagues embarked upon their planned programme of matches for the ensuing season and these were completed on schedule at the end of April the following year. The season saw the Latics finish as runners-up in the First Division, the closest the club has ever come to winning the top flight championship. The club went through a very trying time with Herbert Bamlett, as the team manager and club secretary Mellor volunteering for military service along with many of the club's players.

During these troubled times the club carried on playing regional soccer, relying on a mixture of the old (like Gee and Matthews) and the new (like Everton's Stewart and the deaf-and-dumb Aldred) and in 1918–19 won the Lancashire Subsidiary Tournament "B".

Second World War

In contrast to the events of 1914, once war was declared on 3 September 1939, the Football League programmes of 1939–40 were immediately suspended and the Government forbade any major sporting events so that for a while there was no football of any description.

Oldham's secretary Robert Mellor told the Athletic players that due to international tension their contracts had been terminated. The players, realising that such a position could not be avoided, accepted it philosophically.

During the six years of hostilities, the Latics played in the Northern League.

The club's playing strength at that time was drawn from guest players such as Arthur Buckley (Leeds United), Tommy Butler (Middlesbrough), George Milligan (Everton), Bill Porter (Manchester United) and Tommy Worrall (Portsmouth)—all of whom had previous connections with the club.

Maurice Whittle

Maurice Whittle was recruited from Blackburn Rovers as a wing-half in May 1969, though his early form was very disappointing. In January 1970, he switched to full-back and was an immediate success.

A cool, skilful defender, he built up a fine record for consistency over an eight-year period.

In 1970–71 when the club gained promotion to the Third Division they beat one of the best sides in the Division, a side unbeaten at home for months and months. The Latics played York City off the park, with Maurice Whittle scoring the only goal of the game.

In 1973–74 when the Latics won the Third Division championship, it was Maurice Whittle who cleared a goal-bound effort off the line as Latics held on for a goal-less draw at Plymouth.

Playing his last game for the club in 1977, he then became a part-timer with Wigan Athletic in the Northern Premier League and

after a spell with Fort Lauderdale in the United States, he signed for Barrow. In March 1980, he returned to Wigan after their election to the Football League and went on to play in League games for the 'other' Latics.

From 1970–71 to 1973–74, he missed only one league game out of those four seasons.

His terrific left-foot shot brought him a remarkable number of goals for a full-back, 39 in 312 League appearances for the Latics.

Maurice Whittle—a cool, skilful defender whose terrific left-foot shot brought him a remarkable number of goals for a full-back.

Andrew Wilson

The elder brother of Latics' long-serving wing-half David Wilson, Andrew Wilson began his career in football management with Bristol Rovers in 1921.

Arriving at Boundary Park in July 1927, he will be best remembered for his 1929–30 team which rose from the ashes of near disaster the previous season. The Oldham team line-up still trips of the tongue of today's senior supporters: Hacking, Ivill, Porter, Adlam, King, Goodier, Worrall, Dyson (or Cumming), Littlewood, Gray and Hasson—the teams finished third in Division Two.

When he left Oldham to join Stockport County in the summer of 1932, only four of his successful 1929–30 team remained on the

books—the rest had all been sold without adequate replacement to finance the day-to-day running of the club.

Andrew Wilson had an outstanding playing career. He won six Scottish international caps, two Football League Championship medals and one FA Cup medal with Sheffield Wednesday, for whom he made over 500 appearances in a 20-year association.

Oldham's full league record under Andrew Wilson was:

P	W	D	L	F	A
210	85	44	81	342	333

David Wilson

David Wilson was a wing-half who played in Oldham's very first Football League game against Stoke City on 9 September 1907.

He was a tireless performer whose energy, enthusiasm and sportsmanship allied to his great skill inspired all those who played with him. One of the finest half-backs ever to play for Oldham Athletic, he was a member of the Latics half-back line of Fay, Walders and Wilson that gave many memorable moments.

Surprisingly, his only international appearance was for Scotland in the match against England at Stamford Bridge on 5 April 1913.

He was ever-present when the club finished as runners-up in the First Division in 1915 and one of the stars when Latics were narrowly beaten by Aston Villa in the semi-final of the FA Cup in 1913.

During his time at Boundary Park he set a Football League record of 264 consecutive appearances.

He was a member of a famous footballing family, his brothers being Andrew (Sheffield Wednesday and Scotland and later Latics manager), Alex (Preston North End) and James (St Mirren and Scottish League).

David Wilson was in fact still playing for Nelson in the Second Division at the age of 40. On retirement from the game, he managed Exeter City from March 1928 to February 1929.

Frank Womack

Frank Womack captained Birmingham for 17 consecutive seasons in a 20-year association, subsequently becoming the first player-manager to be appointed in the Birmingham League and leading Worcester City to the championship in his very first season in charge.

After managing Torquay United, he took over the reins at Grimsby Town in May 1932. He led the Mariners into the First Division in 1934, as his side won the Second Division Championship. In October 1936 he moved to Filbert Street to take charge of Leicester City who were lying next to the bottom of Division Two, but at the end of the season they were celebrating a return to the top flight. He remained with the Filberts until the outbreak of war, becoming manager of Notts County in July 1942.

He was appointed manager of Oldham in February 1945, the day that the Soviet Armies advanced to the river Neisse *en route* for Berlin.

The Latics' record in wartime football had been less than impressive, but because of many new signings there was great hope of a serious challenge for promotion when the normal Football League re-opened in 1946–47.

However, quite the reverse happened and in April 1947 Frank Womack resigned. It was a month in which the Latics drew one and lost five matches to finish 19th in the Third Division North, perilously close to having to apply for re-election.

Oldham's full league record under Frank Womack was:

P	W	D	L	F	A
38	10	8	20	53	71

 Ian Wood—current holder of the club's all-time appearances record.

Ian Wood

Ian Wood was signed as an amateur centre-forward by manager Gordon Hurst during the early days of the Latics' youth policy.

He later went on to make several appearances as a promising wing-half, but of course is best remembered for his tremendously energetic and whole-hearted displays at right back. He adopted this position under the management of Jimmy McIlroy.

In the last game of the 1967–68 season he hit all three goals in the club's 3–5 home defeat by Bristol Rovers. That season, he wore seven different numbered shirts, hitting his hat-trick whilst wearing the No. 10.

The Radcliffe-born player was an ever-present in three seasons and from 8 April 1974 played in 232 games, missing just one, a 2–1 defeat at Lincoln on 13 March 1971.

During the close seasons of 1978 and 1979, he was temporarily transferred to San Jose Earthquakes.

Ian Wood was a dedicated long-serving professional, possessing speed, outstanding heading ability and an excellent right foot.

In May 1980 he moved to Turf Moor, thus ending a 14-year association with the Latics, which had seen him pass Dave Wilson's long-standing appearances record. His total of 525 league games is still the club's appearance record.

Billy Wootton

Billy Wootton's appointment as Oldham manager in June 1947 was both unexpected and surprising as he was almost unknown to many followers of the game, coming as he did from Northwich Victoria. Just prior to his appointment, Stan Cullis and Sam Barkas, along with former goalkeeper Jack Hacking were all said to be hot favourites.

As a player, Wootton began his career with Stoke in 1924, followed by a seven-year spell at neighbours Port Vale. He later moved to Southend United, but a knee-injury cut short his league career. However, he recovered enough to join Northwich Victoria as player-

manager and before the outbreak of war the team won both the Cheshire League Challenge Cup, the Cheshire Senior Cup and were finalists in the Edward Case Cup.

After winning only one of their opening 17 league matches, the Latics recovered to finish the 1947–48 season in 11th place. After again starting badly the following season (losing seven of the opening eight matches) sixth place was achieved and 11th in 1949–50.

Billy Wootton did not survive another awful start to 1950–51, resigning after the team had lost six of their first eight matches.

Responsible for the signing of Ray Haddington and Eric Gemmell amongst others, Wootton certainly left the Latics in better shape, both financially and playing-wise. The club cleared a debt of almost £15,000 and had the nucleus of a promotion-challenging side.

Oldham's full league record under Billy Wootton was:

P.	W	D	L	F	A
134	49	34	51	208	212

Workington

Workington joined the Football League in New Brighton's place in 1951–52 and finished bottom of the Third Division North in their first season, though they did inflict upon the Latics one of only two home defeats that season!

They won promotion to the Third Division in 1963–64, a season in which they defeated the Latics 5–3 in the opening round of the League Cup.

Two seasons later they finished fifth in the Third Division, their highest league position, though they failed to the beat the Latics who finished twentieth. Next season, however, they were relegated and stayed in the lower division until losing their League place to Wimbledon in 1976–77.

Zenith Data Systems Cup

The Zenith Data Systems Cup replaced the Simod Cup for the 1989–90 season. Latics first match in this competition saw the club go down 2–0 away to Newcastle United.

When Oldham played at Bramall Lane on 11 December 1990, they raced into a two goal lead and looked as though they were going to go on and score seven. But it was not to be and the strange game that transpired saw the Blades 'keeper in inspired form and the Latics defence hand out more presents than Santa. The final score: Sheffield United 7 Oldham Athletic 2. Even more incredible when the facts reveal that the Yorkshiremen didn't score their opener until twenty minutes had gone and the Latics then went on to concede six more goals in the remaining time.

Drawn at home in 1991–92, the Latics went down 3–2 against Everton with Holden and Milligan getting the goals.